DRAWING THE FUTURE

PAUL STEVENSON OLES

DRAWING THE FUTURE

A DECADE OF ARCHITECTURE IN PERSPECTIVE DRAWINGS

VNR **VAN NOSTRAND REINHOLD COMPANY**
——————————————————— NEW YORK

Printed in the United States of America

Designed by Ernie Haim

Van Nostrand Reinhold Company Inc.
115 Fifth Avenue
New York, New York 10003

Van Nostrand Reinhold Company Limited
Molly Millars Lane
Wokingham, Berkshire RG11 2PY, England

Van Nostrand Reinhold
480 La Trobe Street
Melbourne, Victoria 3000, Australia

Macmillan of Canada
Division of Canada Publishing Corporation
164 Commander Boulevard
Agincourt, Ontario MIS 3C7, Canada

16   15   14   13   12   11   10   9   8   7   6   5   4   3   2   1

Library of Congress Cataloging-in-Publication Data

Oles, Paul Stevenson.
   Drawing the future.

   Includes index.
   1. Oles, Paul Stevenson.   2. Architectural drawing—20th century—
United States.   3. Architectural rendering.   I. Title.
NA2707.044A4   1987   720'.22'2   87-8204
ISBN 0-442-27003-8

This book is dedicated to the poet:

Carole Oles

CONTENTS

FOREWORD

Paul Stevenson Oles draws buildings designed by other architects. But he is no more just a renderer or delineator or "perspectivist," as he prefers to call his profession, than Yehudi Menuhin, say, is simply a performer of other people's musical scores. Both are artists.

Both Oles and Menuhin render or perform another's art with fidelity. Yet both contribute more than the virtuosity of craftsmanship. We say of performing artists that their artistry lies in the way they interpret the work of the composer—the way they bring it to life, and stir the emotions of the audience. A Menuhin evokes qualities in a sonata that the composer may not have known it had. Such is the power of the *Zeitgeist* that a few decades ago, or a few decades hence, the same work of art may be interpreted quite differently by artists who swear they do no more than most faithfully carry out the composer's intentions.

But architecture? Can one interpret not the esoteric meaning, but the physical appearance of a completed architectural design? Each detail of the design is prescribed. The delineator cannot put more feeling into the parapet, play the granite veneer softly and the doorways *adagio*.

The virtuosity of Oles's craftsmanship is not disputed. He prides himself on the accuracy of his work, based on his thorough investigation of all the visual implications of a design. And he is often asked by architects to work with them on shaping the design before he draws it. But whether he helps with the building design or not, his visualization of the project, often prepared years before the groundbreaking, shows exactly how the building will look when completed. Oles's colored rendering of I. M. Pei's East Building of the National Gallery of Art, for instance, is virtually interchangeable with photographs of the actual building, colors and all. The Cambridge Seven Associates's New England Aquarium in Boston is another striking example. You have to look closely to distinguish Oles's vivid preview from a photograph taken from the same vantage point after the dedication.

However, Oles's renderings are often more faithful images of the finished building than photographs are. Not that he would ever put make-up on a building design to enhance its appeal, let alone idealize it. Yet his drawings are often more "architectural" than photographs can be. Oles's informed eye and skilled hand are better able to convey the spirit, or "the intellectual substance of the design," to use I. M. Pei's words, than a camera lens. Thus, his craftsmanship is elevated beyond technique into art.

One of the many refreshing aspects of Oles's work is that, in contrast to some architects these days, he sees and delineates buildings in context, as a part of their environment. Most architects, to be sure, talk a lot about context; it has become a buzz word in the profession. But the more architects discuss the importance of context and "human scale," the less, it seems, they are willing to heed their words. Oles takes context seriously. He would not show us a building in aloof isolation from the "real world," as it is called. He puts people, cars, and other everyday elements into the picture. More important, he also shows, or at least suggests, the new building's relationship to its neighbors, its impact on the cityscape.

His ability to communicate clearly, truthfully, and dramatically has made Oles the profession's favorite architectural renderer, according to a December 1986 survey by *Progressive Architecture*. But beyond popularity, his contributions to architectural design, design philosophy, and education, together with his influence on some of the most important designs of our time, are winning him an increasingly important place in architectural history.

For example, Oles was largely responsible for preserving the integrity of Maya Ying Lin's original competition-winning design of the Vietnam Veterans Memorial in Washington, D.C. Although a distinguished jury clearly saw the great power of her design, selecting it above some fourteen hundred other entries, the sponsoring veterans were at first bewildered by her sketchy, impressionistic pastel drawing, to say nothing of the fact that a twenty-one-year-old undergraduate of Chinese descent was to design an emotion-charged national monument next to the Lincoln Memorial. Some critics rather viciously attacked the design for its abstract character and lack of obvious patriotic metaphor.

Oles recognized the purity and simplicity of Lin's image and resisted pressures to incorporate in his drawing minor design changes that Lin had not authorized. He rendered it, faithfully as always, with such visual eloquence that even those who had not immediately appreciated the merits of the design were won over, including people who felt predisposed against simple modernism.

I. M. Pei's design of the new underground space below the inner court of the Louvre is another of Oles's delineation triumphs. The design calls for glass pyramids (one large one surrounded by small ones) in the interior court to light and shelter the grand entrance to the remodeled museum's subterranean central hall. There was fierce opposition to the pyramids, which, in contrast to obelisks, seemed alien to many Parisians. Oles's drawing shows the "Egyptian intruders" as part of the background—an almost casual adornment—in a perspective that focuses on the rich beauty of the old palace. And that, no doubt, is how Pei's pyramids will be seen and admired now that Pei's grand scheme is being built.

This book includes these and other notable architectural projects undertaken between 1976 and 1986. It is an encouraging book. It is encouraging, for one, to see architectural drawing raised to a practical art of superlative quality. Before Oles came along, architectural drawings—slick advertising aside—tended to be either practical or artistic. They were often imprecise and distorted the truth or tended to show hazy visions and bizarre fanta-

sies, seemingly bent on persuading us that architecture is an art of personal expression, when it should be a social art.

Paul Stevenson Oles's perspectives show us that it can—indeed, that it must—be both: that practical truth can also be poetic; that visual poetry can also be practical.

Architecture students should be the foremost beneficiaries of his approach. They could learn the benefits of drawing, which Oles learned at Texas Tech and Yale, and now teaches at Harvard. Much of his thought on the importance of drawing in the conceptual design process is presented in his 1979 work *Architectural Illustration: The Value Delineation Process,* also published by Van Nostrand Reinhold. When you learn to draw, Oles says, you learn to see, to observe—and to gain knowledge of the world for which you want to design. This is why architecture students two or three generations ago were rarely seen without their sketchbooks. They sketched and drew what they needed to know about the world so they would be able to design a better one. Today they snap pictures.

A further encouragement is the future Oles has drawn. Given the fashionable architectural faddists who dominate the press and some of our skylines, it is cheering to see how many fine buildings will be part of the world to come, as well as how good the buildings are.

And yes, architecture, too, like musical scores, can be interpreted in subtle ways. How? In the end, it's the warmth of the human hand that does it. It is the unique way a Menuhin wields his bow and an Oles wields his pencils.

WOLF VON ECKARDT

INTRODUCTION

The future, it could be argued, is the true medium of the designer. The future to which I refer is not the predictive speculation of the professional futurist nor the fictive dream of the visionary but the definable extension of the present, which forms the raw material available to the practicing artist in design. As a medium, this elusive raw material must be rendered palpable, manipulable, and visible.

To work effectively with any visible medium, the artist must be able to see it with clarity and precision. Despite our amazing advances in the fields of electronics, cybernetics, and photography, the traditional hand-finished representational perspective drawing remains an essential means of providing a clear vision of that future. This book includes a sampling of such drawing, executed particularly to describe the work of predominantly American architects from 1976 to 1986.

Precise and objective architectural drawings of the type assembled here are doubly useful to the realization of sensitive architecture. In addition to providing a means of previsualizing a tentative proposal for further professional study and modification, the drawings communicate the final intentions of the architect to the client, building officials, financial supporters, potential users, and the public at large. While it may be obvious that drawing for communication with the public should be representational—that is, "photographic"—it is generally assumed that much more cryptic drawing should be sufficient for the trained eye of the professional. However, although all sorts of two-dimensional study methods, including schematic drawing, freehand sketching, and computer graphics, have their uses as appropriate design tools, it is the carefully made predictive drawing of a building in its context that finally verifies the wholeness of the architect's vision.

The drawings included in this book share three characteristics. First, all were executed between 1976 and 1986. Second, each drawing has been executed in the medium of wax-base pencil, according to the principles of the value delineation system, as described in my book *Architectural Illustration* (also published by Van Nostrand Reinhold). Third, at the time of execution, each drawing depicted some future construction. Depending on when one reads this book, those structures may remain to be built in the future, may be part of the present, or may even have been razed. Some projects, of course, will never be realized, which leaves the image as communicated by the drawing as the historically definitive one for that particular work.

With all their similarities, there are certainly differences among the drawings. Some show the placing of a small, new element in an existing context (such as the Louvre), while others show the completion of a building already under construction (as in the Washington Cathedral), and still others deal only with internal contextural demands (for example, the Portland Museum section perspectives). Most of the drawings were executed in black-and-white, although a few were drawn as color originals. Some other achromatic drawings had color added to a photographic print according to a process that I call "retrocolor." (A number of the color drawings reproduced here in black-and-white may be seen in their full-color versions in a forthcoming Van Nostrand Reinhold book about color in architectural illustration by Harold Linton and Richard Rochon.)

The hundred drawings included here represent sixty-one architectural projects; they are grouped into six chapters according to project location. The order of drawings within each section is approximately chronological. Several drawings describe projects designed by my office, but most were commissioned by other architects primarily for the purpose of public representation of their designs. In several cases drawings are paired, allowing the investigation and comparison of day/night or other variations. Multiple views of the same project enable the two-dimensional page to communicate not only the third dimension (space) but the fourth (time) as well.

Accompanying each drawing is a commentary describing my intentions and the way in which that particular work fulfilled or failed to fulfill them. Every undertaking presents its challenges, demands, and opportunities, and each of these drawings carries its own set of lessons. The commentaries are intended to provide the most useful information possible for those concerned with creating or understanding representational architectural drawings.

A drawing of the future has at least two potential lives. First, it provides a useful predictive image of an unbuilt project; it then becomes an artifact in its own right after the building has been constructed. Whereas standard exterior and interior views tend to be relegated to the realm of historical documents by photographs of the actual building after its completion, some drawings (such as section perspectives) can never be replicated by photography. These drawings are assembled here not only to provide a glimpse of a decade of architectural accomplishment but also in the hope that they will continue to have meaning as works of art even after the future they represent has become history.

DRAWING THE FUTURE

1 New England Projects

Dracut Housing for the Elderly (Competition)

This drawing of our own design of a housing project for the elderly was originally published in my first book, *Architectural Illustration,* in 1979. It is a final drawing of the scheme prior to construction, and shows the project approximately as it was built in its rural setting. It may be interesting to compare the duotone image printed here with the standard monotone, or single-color, reproduction of the earlier book.

A common problem of composition in the eye-level illustration of a widely spaced scheme of units such as this one is excessive horizontality. This format is almost two squares in proportion, yet it encompasses less than half of the project—with the buildings occupying only a narrow horizontal band in the center. A common solution, used here, is to include discretionary elements, such as trees, to counter the otherwise unrelieved horizontality. One way to ameliorate the compositional necessity of showing a great expanse of foreground is to choose a viewpoint that places something interesting (water, in this case) in that foreground.

The pond shown here, reclaimed from a swamp as part of the project design, became a constructed amenity, which the drawing features. The trees and foreground cattails were drawn over a watercolor paper underlay to increase drawing speed and coarseness of the texture, so that the eye would not be caught up in details of elements that are only incidental to the building.

You may notice that this drawing is identified by our office logotype. Other drawings are identified by name and year, and some lack any identifying mark at all. Drawings made entirely or nearly entirely by my own hand are typically signed, whereas drawings that involved substantial staff contribution carry the logotype. Projects designed by our office are also marked by the logo—usually solid rather than open—as in this case. Drawings used for competition entry have no identification whatever, to ensure the competitor's anonymity. Other drawings showing no mark at all may simply be the victims of cropping.

Dracut, Massachusetts
The Lowe/Interface Partnership
Exterior perspective
Black Prismacolor on 100% rag bond (with partial textural underlay)
10" × 7"
Three days (1977)

Massachusetts State Transportation Building

This major downtown Boston design was so extensive that the only way to show it in its entirety, and in its particular urban context, was with an aerial view, which is included here as an inset. This drawing is an example of a photomontage "cut-in" procedure, which is described on page 6 in connection with the following project. The impact of the Transportation building from eye level was, of course, important as well, so this "driver's-eye view" was chosen to emphasize the gentle curve of the major façade. Notice that the darkness of the brick changes at the curve (because of the change in the incident angle of sunlight on the façade, further dramatizing the gradual change in plane.

City context in the eye-level view is provided by four identifiable Boston buildings, including the old and new Hancock towers, which also appear in the drawing of the Heritage Condominium project later in this chapter. The building on the near corner in the right side of the drawing has been "finessed," or deleted, to show the near façade of the new project—albeit mostly through a lacy screen of trees.

The foreground trees were created, for the most part, subtractively. That is, their foliage is mainly a product of erasure—specifically of an electric erasing machine with a vinyl insert sharpened to a point, which I sometimes refer to as the "negative pencil." On another technical note, the thin crosswalk lines in the street intersection were produced by a process that I call "scoring," but others sometimes describe as the impressed line technique. It involves making an identation in the paper or board with some pointed (but not sharp) instrument such as a leather tool before value is applied; the line then appears as white after the application of value, which cannot reach the paper in the indented trough. This simple drawing technique greatly facilitates a graphic task that would be much more time consuming and less precise if done in the conventional manner.

Boston, Massachusetts
Goody, Clancy & Associates
Exterior perspective
Black Prismacolor on Strathmore board
14" × 18"
Seven days (1978)

This aerial photomontage drawing by the author shows the relationship of the building to downtown Boston.

Connecticut General Life Insurance Headquarters

The three illustrations of this project shown represent only the last stage of a long, careful design process in which investigatory drawing was integral from the beginning. Dozens of studies of alternative schemes, sitings, and details were drawn and presented over several years before this final proposal was reached. Most of the earlier sketches and drawings had been produced in black-and-white, but these are color originals, which may explain the slight haze that may be evident in the black-and-white reproduction.

The aerial view of the project seeks to show, in very straightforward terms, the relationship of the proposed and existing parts of this corporate headquarters complex. In order to avoid redrawing the existing part, we used a photomontage technique, which involves mounting a photograph (with rubber cement) to high-quality drawing board, then cutting out a precise window for the new part of the drawing. The window should be as "ragged" as possible, integrating many elements of the photograph into the new area of drawing. In this case, foreground trees in the photograph were saved to enclose the new drawing area more completely within the photographic image.

The plants, pool, waterfall, and light quality indicated in the interior view of the atrium are intended to suggest the ambiance of the proposed space. Color was used to make some distinctions that have disappeared in this achromatic reproduction—notably the third person in the central group of figures. It is virtually impossible to make a subtle color drawing that will translate, without some loss of definition, into a black-and-white image, but the opposite effect, "retrocoloring," is quite a bit simpler to achieve, as it simply involves applying color to a printed image.

The exterior eye-level drawing is a fairly direct, straightforward view of a long, low building. As in the earlier Dracut drawing, trees are the vertical compositional elements used to keep the viewer's gaze contained within the format. The foreground tree shadow and stone wall add a convenient dark base to the arrangement of graphic elements, and increase the stability of the entire composition.

Bloomfield, Connecticut
The Architects Collaborative (J. Harkness)
Aerial perspective (photomontage)
Black Prismacolor on Strathmore board
16" × 20"
Four days (1978)

(page 8)
Interior perspective
Prismacolor on Strathmore board
11½" × 15"
Seven days (1978)

(page 9)
Exterior perspective
Prismacolor on Strathmore board
13" × 16"
Seven days (1978)

Middlebury College Alumni Conference Center

Here is an example of an interior perspective drawing composed of simple elements, with the exception of the folded hyperbolic roof, a trademark of this particular architect. Value delineation, or tone drawing, is ideally suited to show the warped planes of the ceiling; tonal gradation reinforces the linear cues provided by the joints in the wood decking. The decking members are also defined by slightly varying the tone of occasional planks in the manner frequently seen in actual construction.

The means of lighting this space—always a major factor in the drawing of an interior perspective—is primarily natural. The intensity of natural daylight is so much greater than that of artificial lighting that the illumination from fixtures in a daytime view can often be totally disregarded in a drawing. In this case, most light enters the space through the large areas of glazing seen in the picture, although minor amounts of light are admitted from openings behind the observer. The outside scene visible through these windows is severely "overexposed," as would be the case in a typical daytime photograph of the space.

This brings to our attention a dilemma of value drawing that is so common that it bears mentioning here. That paradox involves the decision of how dark to show the wall area immediately surrounding the bright exterior view as seen from an interior. Physics would predicate that the area of ceiling nearest the window would be most brightly lighted, but principles of perceptual psychology dictate that we see areas immediately adjacent to great brightness as very dark indeed. This is particularly true in the case of small members, such as mullions, surrounded by high glare. Even if the dividing members in the glazed wall shown here were actually white, a normal-exposure photograph would render them virtually black.

It is not necessary, of course, to accept and be strictly bound by all the constraints of photography in a drawing. However, as a culture conditioned by photographs and other light-sensitive replications of form, we find "photographic" images to be highly credible and universally legible—both qualities usually considered very positive in an architectural illustration.

Middlebury, Vermont
Daniel F. Tully Associates
Interior perspective
Black Prismacolor on 100% rag bond
8½" × 11"
Three days (1978)

Holiday Inn Proposal

These two drawings illustrate one of the many hotel proposals made for Boston during the 1970s. The drawings relate the tower building to the existing urban context, and show the character of the street-level spaces as seen from the exterior.

The exterior (daytime) drawing viewpoint was chosen to include a range of existing buildings along the right half of the drawing, and that most potent of modern urban landmarks, the Boston City Hall, on the left. An afternoon sun angle was chosen, which leaves the visible wall of City Hall in shade, thereby suppressing some of the potentially distracting façade detail. The huge shadow cast by the building provides a convenient means to include the dependable and effective compositional device of the dark foreground. Again, this reduces the number of visual elements that could compete with and vitiate the impact of the proposed building.

The inclusion of the two tall lighting standards raises a question fairly common in architectural illustration: to what degree should liberty be taken to "clean up" a scene by eliminating noncrucial or incidental elements? We decided to include incidental elements in this drawing, judging that they would not be too distracting, but have opted in other cases not to do so, as in the Portland Museum project shown later in this chapter. The shorter lighting standards with double globes are clearly part of an urban design intention, and therefore their inclusion was not in question.

The detail view of the building was couched in twilight for two reasons. First, early evening is a time of day when hotel activities might be at a peak and second, twilight offers to photographers and illustrators the compelling opportunity to show a building with its daytime personality (exterior form defined against the sky) and its nighttime personality (dramatically visible interior spaces) simultaneously. Glazing is shown here as primarily transparent, as is nearly always the case with night views, but some sky reflections can be seen in the glazed awnings. The presence of these two kinds of cues reminds the viewer of the transparent and reflective nature of glass.

Boston, Massachusetts
Cambridge Seven Associates (P. Chermayeff)
Exterior perspective (general view)
Black Prismacolor on Strathmore board
17" × 20"
Five days (1979)

(page 14)
Exterior perspective (detail view)
Black Prismacolor on Strathmore board
12" × 18"
Five days (1979)

MIT Arts and Media Technology Building

This pair of illustrations provides information on the design process in addition to showing the building. The drawing of the preliminary scheme places the structure in the context of adjacent MIT buildings—a dormitory on the right and the Pei-designed chemical engineering building on the left—and seeks to explain the presence of the gateway, which celebrates the main circulation axis of the institute. The Venturi-designed building seen beyond completes the homage to this axis.

The principal material of the preliminary scheme was to have been 4-foot-square aluminum panels—a challenging material to illustrate convincingly, particularly when viewed straight on. Its diffusely reflective quality produced a wall that was dark from the horizon down, and much lighter in the portion reflecting sky. This particular sky was probably drawn too dark and too coarsely textured, but it was intended to be a dramatic foil for the very smooth and somewhat lightish building. Note the sunlight "deflections" from the unseen glass situated between the two major building walls.

The later (1981) drawing shows a building considerably transformed, now sheathed in white, semireflective metal panels with ribbon glazing. The gate structure, now freestanding, provides an ideal element to cue the varying reflective levels of wall panels and glazing strongly. The orientation of the structure predicated that the major wall seen from this viewpoint would almost always be in shade. Since it is a totally planar wall, no shadow opportunities are lost by this constraint and a fairly dramatic sunshade definition of the two visible walls is achieved. In the color version of this drawing the shade side is shown as quite blue, because of the facts that it reflects blue sky on one hand, and is illuminated by diffuse blue sky light on the other.

Cambridge, Massachusetts
I. M. Pei & Partners (I. M. Pei)
(page 16)
Exterior perspective (preliminary scheme)
Black Prismacolor on vellum with watercolor paper underlay
15" × 20"
Six days (1979)

(page 17)
Exterior perspective (final scheme)
Prismacolor on Strathmore board
12" × 19"
Seven days (1981)

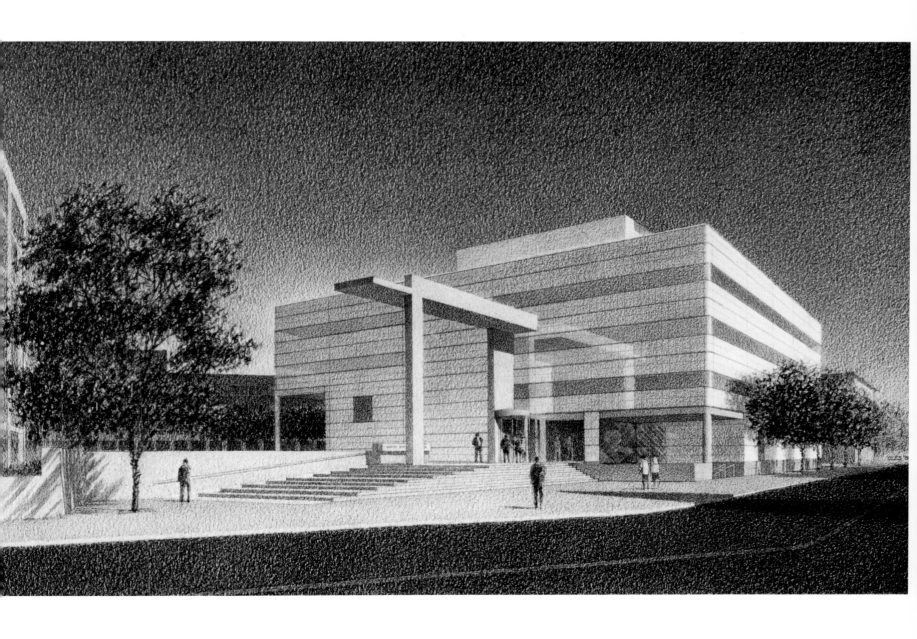

Portland Museum of Art

The Portland Museum of Art, designed by Henry Nichols Cobb of I. M. Pei & Partners, is a building conceived with rigor and care. Technically an addition, but actually larger than the original museum, which consisted of a series of residential-scale buildings, the new structure was designed to serve the double function of housing the exhibitions and providing an urban presence to complete an otherwise inchoate public space called Congress Square.

This (color original) exterior drawing illustrates the relationship of the new project to the existing neighboring buildings in Congress Square. The clock tower of the building at the right is obviously an important landmark, and had to be included in the drawing although it required an enormous amount of sky, which unfortunately diminished the percentage of the format occupied by the new building. The cylindrical tower is located well beyond the limit of the 60 degree cone of vision and becomes quite distorted in the constructed drawing. We have taken the liberty of reducing somewhat the degree of distortion in the final drawing, as you may observe by comparing it with the inset photograph.

The exterior view was constructed from a station point that was carefully selected for its future accessibility in order to make this corresponding photograph of the completed building. The location and design of the street and signal-light standards were not available at the time of the 1979 drawing. Even if they had been known, a strong case might have been made for their deletion or at least graphic suppression because of their visual distraction. As you may observe, the cluster of birch trees in front of the building is shown in a somewhat more mature state of development than is evident in the photograph, which was taken shortly after the building was completed in 1983.

The interior design of the building is a study in the careful manipulation of natural light admitted by octagonal lanterns and allowed to filter, diffuse, and bounce through the various spaces. The section perspective in value delineation is the ideal drawing combination to show the building's subtle interplay of light, structure, and space. The monochromatic transverse and longitudinal drawings appearing on the following pages give a remarkably accurate sense of the interior hierarchy of light and space, based on observation and photographs of the building in actual use.

Portland, Maine
I. M. Pei & Partners (H. Cobb)
Exterior perspective
Prismacolor on Strathmore board
14" × 22"
Nine days (1979)

(page 20)
Section perspective (longitudinal)
Black Prismacolor and ink on Strathmore board
14" × 22"
Six days (1981)

(page 21)
Section perspective (transverse)
Black Prismacolor and ink on Strathmore board
14" × 22"
Six days (1980)

This photograph by Steve Rosenthal shows the completed building from the same viewpoint as the preconstruction drawing. (Photograph © 1983 Steve Rosenthal.)

The Heritage Condominiums

It was the shared intention of the architect, the developer, and the perspectivist that this drawing clearly communicate the major intent of this carefully crafted design to be sympathetic and responsive to the urban context in which the building was sited. A certain vagueness or sketchiness was deemed appropriate (to harmonize with impressionist paintings used elsewhere in the marketing brochure), as was the use of color.

A specific sense of location was established by the inclusion of three landmark buildings that would be recognizable to any Bostonian. The foreground is provided by the Public Garden, which forms, along with the Boston Common, the green heart of the city. In the original version color also helped define the sense of place, suggesting the use of the typical Boston red brick as the principal material of construction.

The choice of viewpoint in the Public Garden posed something of a problem; showing the many trees in full summer foliage would block most of the view of the building. A winter scene with skeletal trees and snow might have been effective (see the New England Sunbox project) but that was judged to be somewhat bleak. We opted for early spring as the season of choice, as it allowed building visibility along with green grass and the first touch of green buds in the tree branches. A common solution to the problem of obscuring trees is simply to delete them from the drawing, but to remove large, familiar trees from this location would have sent entirely the wrong message.

The tree versus building dilemma, so common in architectural drawing and photography, almost never poses a problem in actuality. In experiencing a building, we perceive it from a continuum of viewpoints, not merely from the single point in time and space required for conventional graphic representation.

Boston, Massachusetts
The Architects Collaborative (H. Elkus)
Exterior perspective
Prismacolor on tan illustration board
12" × 20"
Six days (1983)

New England Sunbox (Competition)

These three drawings were part of an entry submission to a design competition for energy-efficient single-family houses, sponsored by a regional utility company. The design was selected as one of three that were eventually constructed on various sites across New England.

The exterior drawing shows an eye-level view of the house, complementing a detailed model that was also part of the entry requirements. The choice of a snow scene seemed natural to New England and, pragmatically, reduced the drawing time by the elimination of most foreground features. To emphasize the warmth and coziness of the house as "home," I showed the weary father and son crosscountry skiers returning to, no doubt, a steaming cup of hot chocolate prepared by the welcoming mother seen on the greenhouse deck.

The design is for a passive solar house, but a fireplace and masonry chimney are included as an auxiliary heat source and for thermal storage. That raised the question of whether the chimney should be shown emitting smoke (a sign that the solar heat storage capacity was insufficient?) or should be indicated as dormant with a neat little blanket of snow perched on top. The discerning eye might see my indecision, betrayed by the hazy streak fading off to the right as part of the sky, or possibly a wisp of woodsmoke.

The greenhouse, or sunspace, drawing illustrates the house's only architecturally unusual feature in a simple horizontal perspective view. I was most interested in constructing and rendering the fading superimposed (transmitted and reflected) images shown through and beyond the glazed sliding doors on the right.

The interior view, taken from a kitchen pass-through, shows those same doors from the inside. This drawing is intended to convey the sense of looking out through two walls of glass enclosing an area of planting. In this section, the exterior scene (with snow outside or not) would appear very brilliant against the much less brightly illuminated interior surfaces. Reflections in floor, table, and countertop materials seemed to add interest and depth to the picture. Actual photographs taken later from this viewpoint verified quite satisfactorily the graphic assumptions illustrated here.

Methuen, Massachusetts
Interface Architects (P. S. Oles)
Exterior perspective
Black Prismacolor on vellum with partial textural underlay
12" × 17"
Two days (1983)

(page 26)
Interior perspective (sun space)
Black Prismacolor on vellum with textural underlay
16" × 16"
Two days (1983)

(page 27)
Interior perspective (dining room)
Black Prismacolor on vellum with textural underlay
Two days (1983)

This photograph by the author shows a slightly modified Sunbox prototype situated in Methuen, Massachusetts.

2 New York Projects

New York, New York
Cambridge Seven Associates (Bruce Kelly with Philip N. Winslow, ASLA)
Exterior perspective
Black Prismacolor and Verithin pencil on Mylar
7" × 9½"
Three days (1978)

(page 30)
Interior perspective (entrance space)
Black Prismacolor on vellum
7" × 9½"
Four days (1978)

(page 31)
Interior perspective (exhibition space)
Black Prismacolor on vellum
8" × 10"
Three days (1978)

New York Public Library Rehabilitation

Two of these three drawings were originally published in my 1979 book *Architectural Illustration* in standard monotone reproduction. They are printed here in duotone. Anyone concerned with the graphic fidelity of the printing process may be interested in comparing the image quality of the two publications.

The exterior view is printed here at slightly larger than actual size, from a wax-base pencil drawing on Mylar. The main purpose of the illustration was to show a range of proposed landscaping modifications. The layout was traced over a photograph of the building taken in 1977 by Norman McGrath. Although the photograph was taken during the winter, we changed the seasonal context to summer to show the landscaping elements in their most resplendent form.We also chose the vignette format and diminished the resolution of surrounding buildings to feature the exquisite Beaux-Arts detail of the library building itself.

On page 30, the drawing of the main entry foyer shows the space almost as it existed, with only minor design alterations, such as the information booth the designers added under the stair. The purpose of this illustration is somewhat unusual—to show how little impact the proposed design elements will have on an existing space.

The third view is of an interior exhibition space, showing the location and unobtrusive character of several proposed display cases. The purpose of this drawing is similar to the previous one, to celebrate a noble interior space—which was almost completely obscured by makeshift lighting fixtures and temporary partitions when design work and drawings were underway.

We thought it would be particularly important to illustrate the floor material and pattern with care. By assuming that the space would be illuminated primarily by natural light from windows along the left side of the picture, we saw that the near side of the arches would be quite dark. The reflected images of these strong dark shapes provided a good opportunity to show the reflective patina of this handsome stone floor.

499 Park Avenue Tower

This photomontage drawing was commissioned as a promotional piece for a developer's speculative office building, built in New York at the end of the 1970s. As with any project of this type, location was considered to be of primary importance. The Park Avenue address was a major selling point, and to reinforce this notion I wanted to show the building situated as closely as possible to the "center" of the Avenue—that is, the neighborhood of Grand Central Station and the Pan Am building.

With this in mind, I photographed the existing scene with a 35mm perspective-correcting lens, then printed only the central part of the picture to achieve the compressing effect of a much longer focal-length lens. The resulting image showed Pan Am as closer to the new building than the full-frame photograph would have done.

The constructed geometry of the building was quite simple to verify, as the plans and elevations of the surrounding buildings were available. Fully as important to the drawing of this mirror-glazed tower was the construction of adjacent building reflections. Although this was done with a great deal of care, there is one error of reflection here that will be apparent to the truly observant critic.

The actual rendering of the building was done with the "cut-in" technique described on page 6. The upper parts of the two major planes of the building are very different in value even though both reflect sky. The main reason for the difference is that the angle of view to the right façade is *raking* (at a very small angle with the surface) and to the left facade is near *normal* (approximately perpendicular). The raking view glances off the surface of the glazing and almost completely reflects the light sky, whereas the normal view penetrates it to a greater degree—even though the glass is partially mirrored—and reaches to the relative darkness of the interior spaces.

Although the architect was pleased with the precise way in which the proposed building was shown in context, the developer, deciding that building had become too "incidental," eventually opted to market the project with a model photograph of the building alone, shown in no context whatever.

New York, New York
I. M. Pei & Partners (J. Freed)
Perspective view down Park Avenue (photomontage)
Black Prismacolor on Strathmore board
20" × 16"
Five days (1978)

900 Third Avenue Tower

Although it is usually more dramatic as well as democratic to show an urban tower from the pedestrian's eye level, we chose a higher viewpoint in this case in order to show as much of the building as possible. We also had access to a photograph of the site that had been taken from an adjacent building—a perfect contextural document to use as an underlay. The perspective construction of the new building was made, therefore, to fit the station point and the size of the photograph.

If you look closely, you can observe a great deal of graphic activity in and on the façade of the tower. As with the Dallas Centre project (see chapter 4) there are two kinds of façades interlaced within the building face: one is the matte spandrel, and the other is reflective glazing. This duality yields a surprising degree of graphic richness as a result of simply determining and rendering with care the reflected building in the ribbons of glazing, and the effect of sun, shade, and shadow on the bands of spandrel.

Although the reflections are carefully constructed, some liberty was taken to move their edges slightly when necessary to reduce ambiguity. For instance, the tops of low buildings reflected in the façade are typically shown as terminating in the glazing bands where they may be seen, rather than between them. Also, the shadow of an adjacent tall building that falls on the right-hand façade was moved so it would not quite coincide with the reflected edge of another tower. To some extent, these graphic elements can, and I believe should, be "composed."

Another discretionary element of composition is the sky, which, in the tradition of Pelli's own fine drawing, is used freely to provide graphic foil where it will benefit the drama or legibility of the drawing. I have made liberal use of the device of "aura" here to isolate the building graphically to some extent, particularly toward the lower right side where important formal gestures would otherwise be lost against identical adjacent values.

One final element of the façade that enriches (and complicates) the drawing is the area of aluminum spandrel introduced to match the low element of the Citicorp Center seen in the foreground. Notice that the major shadow on the right façade changes value as it crosses the aluminum, but the tone of the glazing above and below the material is constant, since shadow is not visible on glass.

New York, New York
Cesar Pelli & Associates
Exterior perspective
Black Prismacolor on Strathmore board
16½″ × 11½″
Eight days (1980)

Jacob K. Javits Convention Center

This series of three drawings of the recently completed Jacob K. Javits Convention Center was commissioned by the architect for general publicity purposes, and for inclusion in an exhibition at the Museum of Modern Art in New York. For that exhibition in the winter of 1981, the drawings were greatly enlarged by photography and the mounted prints were retrocolored with wax-base pencils. In order to achieve the precisely intended color balance, the retrocolor work was done in the museum, under actual final lighting conditions.

The daytime exterior view of this enormous, five-block-long building is taken from 34th Street looking west. Since the building is on the western edge of the city, there is almost no urban development beyond it, making the reflected images of midtown buildings important in placing the Convention Center in a specific context. The virtual (reflected) images of the city were constructed with photographs taken from the virtual station point, on the West Side Highway, and printed in reverse.

The nighttime exterior view shows a building of an entirely different character. Since the mirror glazing—reflective by day—is transparent at night, the image of the city disappears and the building skin becomes invisible, exposing the intricacy of the interior structure. Overcast days or twilight are inspiring times to view (and illustrate) the building, as the reflective and transparent nature of the glazing are simultaneously visible.

The interior view shows the largest and highest space of the building, since the entire interior is much too extensive to be encompassed in a single perspective drawing. A nautical exhibition theme was selected for the illustration, as it offered natural choices for scale devices, such as yachts of appropriate size to help establish the enormity of even this fractional part of the building's interior.

The perspective construction of this drawing was itself a considerable feat. Since space frames are precisely definable in space —unlike, for example, trees—the relative darkening of tone against the sky resulting from dozens of overlapping structural members is quite specific and predictable. In order to indicate this darkening with any precision, however, each member must be plotted and drawn. This would be virtually impossible on a single construction drawing, so we used the devices of color-coded line and registered overlay construction sheets (seven, to be exact) to construct the visible forest of nodes and struts. Here is a case in which computer-generated perspective construction clearly would have been the method of choice, but the facilities were not available to us at that time.

New York, New York
I. M. Pei & Partners (J. Freed)
Interior perspective
Black Prismacolor on Strathmore board
20" × 20"
Thirteen days (1979)

(page 38)
Exterior perspective (day view)
Black Prismacolor on Strathmore board (retrocolored)
16" × 24"
Nine days (1979)

(page 39)
Exterior perspective (night view)
White Prismacolor on black museum board (retrocolored)
16" × 24"
Eight days (1979)

This photograph by the author shows the main space of the convention center on its opening day in April 1986.

Bulova Watch Factory Rehabilitation Proposal

This Long Island condominium design is a rehabilitation of a former watch factory building. To show in a single drawing the several kinds of spaces included—exterior, interior, cortile, and swimming pool—the section perspective seemed to be the only alternative.

As highly descriptive as the section perspective may be, some kinds of information are difficult for it to convey accurately. For example, in glancing at this drawing one would assume that the building is entirely orthogonal in plan. In fact, the right-hand wing cut by the section line is at a greater-than-90-degree angle to the rest of the building. That means that the cut line through that wing showing the internal spaces is not perpendicular to the axis of the wing. This can be verified by observing that the width of the building appears greater in the right wing than in the left (they are in fact equal) and the mullions in the roof skylight are not parallel to the cut line. Although nothing crucial is lost by these slight ambiguities, it reminds us that care should be exercised in the selection and reading of even this most informative drawing type.

The cortile space offers a perennial problem facing illustrators of space frames in sunlight: whether to show the shadows of frame members on the surfaces within the space. I have found that the assumption of a hazy sky is almost always the best one to make, both to improve descriptive clarity and increase drawing speed. Accordingly, we have shown shadows as very soft-edged, particularly in the cortile where only the beginnings of shadows are depicted falling from the space frame and wall intersections. The somewhat sharper tree shadows drawn across exterior walls may seem a bit inconsistent, but it could be claimed that the acrylic skylights diffuse some of the light falling within the cortile.

Although it may be a bit difficult to detect, given the size of this reproduction, this drawing was one of our first to receive tuning and texture modification through a knife-scratching procedure sometimes referred to as *sgraffito*. This technique is discussed on page 42, in connection with the New York Botanical Gardens project.

Sag Harbor, New York
Croxton Collaborative
Section perspective
Black Prismacolor on Strathmore board (retrocolored)
12½" × 21½"
Five days (1981)

New York Botanical Gardens Addition

This drawing seeks to show how compatible a proposed addition to a building can be with the original, existing structure. The new library portion, on the left, was designed virtually to replicate much of the detail and rhythm of the existing building, so the task of showing compatibility was considerably simplified in this case.

Both the eye-level viewpoint and sun angle had to be carefully selected in order to show the somewhat distant entrance, which we positioned intentionally in the center of the format. By showing sunlight as raking the façades normal to our view, we were able to show the entrance situated between the dark foreground wall on the right and the bright receding wall of the addition on the left. The reverse arrangement, tested with an alternative value study, might have worked almost as well, but the existing tulip tree in the center is defined more clearly against a light wall.

The tulip tree and the one on the extreme right of the picture were carefully drawn from several available photographs, while the smaller trees did not exist when the drawing was made. The extensive use of a watercolor paper underlay facilitated the rendering of foliage and its shadow a well as parts of the sky and foreground showing a fairly vigorous texture. Varying methods of manipulating the pencil, which are explained in detail in *Architectural Illustration,* allow the production of a wide range of textures, even with the presence of the coarse underlay.

This drawing shows extensive use throughout the format of a recently adopted scratch technique called *sgraffito*. Sgraffito is a useful, effective means of subtractive tuning in which the tip of a very sharp X-acto knife (my preference is the #11 blade) is repeatedly whisked across a troublesome, too-dark area of the drawing in order to lighten it.

The direction of stroke should be consistently maintained—a right-handed person would probably use the cursive slope, or upper right to lower left—and in this illustration that happily coincides with the direction of incident sunlight as well. This treatment of a drawing seems almost never to damage it, providing that it is done at several places in the format, and it introduces a very manipulable secondary texture that is a substantial aid to drawing coherence.

Bronx, New York
Beckhard Richlan & Associates
Exterior perspective
Black Prismacolor on vellum with textural underlay (retrocolored)
11" × 17"
Six days (1985)

Queens College Library

These three drawings of a proposed library building for Queens College are part of a series of five originals first commissioned for fund-raising purposes, then placed permanently in the college archives. Four of the five were to be retrocolored, with the single exception being the night view shown opposite.

This drawing, like almost all night views produced by this office, is drawn on black board with white wax-base pencil. It is, of course, possible to show color in a night drawing, but I believe the major dramatic impact is usually achieved through the use of *chiaroscuro*—simply the effective arrangement of lights and darks within the format. Color is not so visible in less intense light, and since artificial light is almost always much less intense than sunlight, the inclusion of vivid color in the nighttime illustration of buildings is only occasionally appropriate.

The lighting scheme and consequently the drawing strategy are quite simple and powerful in this picture. Almost all light emanates from the central rotunda, casting all surfaces facing away from it in darkness. This arrangement also sends a spray of light upward, slightly visible against the night sky as a reminder of the building's importance as a campus destination.

The eye-level daytime views shown on the following pages are quite direct in their statements. Both illustrations attempt to show primarily the relationship of the new building to existing and proposed campus landscaping and adjacent structures. Another of the five views, not included here, shows the seven-mile-distant Manhattan skyline as observed from this part of the campus.

The sheathing materials chosen for the building were two varieties of pink granite, one lighter than the other. The play between these two materials—in co-planar banding and in adjacent elements—was thoughtfully addressed in the drawings. Particular care was taken to provide "value constancy" where paired materials turn corners from sunlight into shade. "Value algebra," a systematic method for accurately predicting these sets of tonal changes, is explained in *Architectural Illustration*.

In the left-hand drawing showing the orchard, the common problem of multiple foliated trees obscuring some important architectural feature arose once more. Our solution here was simply to waive illustrative realism, and show the overlapping rows of trees as magically hazy. Surprisingly, this fictive transparency seems to damage the credibility of the picture very little if at all.

Queens, New York
The Gruzen Partnership
Exterior perspective (night view)
White Prismacolor on black museum board
13″ × 18″
Seven days (1985)

(page 46)
Exterior perspective (south view)
Black Prismacolor on vellum drymounted to board (retrocolored)
13″ × 18″
Seven days (1985)

(page 47)
Exterior perspective (east view)
Black Prismacolor on vellum drymounted to board (retrocolored)
13″ × 18″
Seven days (1985)

JFK 2000
(Airport Expansion Proposal)

The "science fiction" quality of this nighttime aerial view makes it perhaps the best example in the book of "drawing the future." The future shown here is surrounded by the present. As many will recognize, the periphery of the complex is the existing ring of terminals comprising the main part of New York's John F. Kennedy airport. The proposed central element, scheduled for completion by the year 2000, is an enormous customs and immigration processing facility designed to accommodate 45 million incoming passengers per year. The facility will be connected to the individual terminals by a pedestrian transportation system.

The appropriateness of a nighttime aerial drawing of this scheme seemed self-evident, for this view simultaneously solved the problems of encompassing the whole complex in one drawing and of showing a design that is necessarily somewhat unresolved in precise architectural detail. This aerial view, it may also be argued, will be among the most memorable of those seen by future travelers from the windows of approaching aircraft. In the twenty-first century, fewer visitors and immigrants to this country will sail past the welcoming symbol of the Statue of Liberty—more will arrive at JFK airport.

The precise determination of the station point was undertaken with great care. Model photographs were studied and determinations of view direction, distance, and altitude were made. Armed with this information, members of the architect's staff and a photographer flew to the site at twilight in a helicopter, and obtained a useful series of photographs from which to work. Rather than speculating about the lighting patterns produced by the various existing terminals, we had photographic proof as well as a precise, full-size graphic underlay with which to construct the existing parts of the view. The proposed facility was constructed from plans, elevations, and a model photograph taken from exactly the same angle as the aerial photographic underlay.

The prediction and rendering of lighting patterns of the proposed facility were carefully matched to the patterns of the existing terminals as observed in the photographs. The amount of moisture in the atmosphere produced a specific degree of flare from single light sources that was carefully replicated for corresponding conditions in the proposed area. Notice the faint suggestion of water beyond the runways of the airport, by the subtle reflection of suburban lights from the far side of the bay.

Queens, New York
I. M. Pei & Partners (H. Cobb)
Aerial perspective (night view)
White Prismacolor on black museum board
16" × 20"
Eight days (1985)

This photograph taken by Nathaniel Lieberman shows the project model from an altitude slightly higher than the one finally selected. (Photograph © Nathaniel Lieberman.)

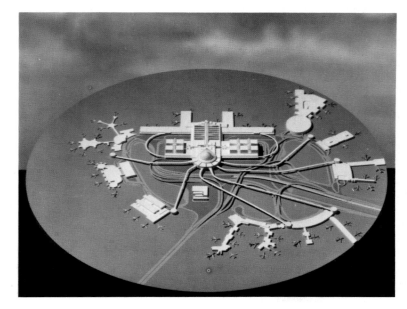

Columbus Center Development

The three views included on these pages are part of a five-drawing series commissioned to describe one of the most ambitious projects undertaken in recent years in New York City. The 70-story asymmetrical twin-tower scheme, located at the southwest corner of Central Park on the site of the former Coliseum is designed to house just about everything—the world headquarters of a major financial corporation, over 200 luxury condominiums, speculative office space, a 400-room hotel, and a retail shopping galleria to compete with any in the city.

Naturally, a project of this scope would be shown by means of at least one architectural model in addition to drawings, which was indeed true in this case. The station points of the five retro-color drawings were selected to show views impossible to obtain from observing or photographing the models, which explains the absence of drawings showing overall exterior views.

The most generally descriptive drawing of the heart of the scheme is the section perspective shown opposite. The view is of the complex sheared in half, as it were, looking toward the north with the Gulf + Western building and Central Park on the right. It was deemed particularly important by the architect and the developer to show more urban context than usual in the section perspective because of the importance of the location to the project. It may be interesting to compare this drawing with the two section perspectives of the Portland Museum, which are shown entirely devoid of exterior context.

The pair of drawings on the following pages are unusual for my office in that they are perspectives with vertical vanishing points, one with the viewer looking up, the other down. They are not true triaxial or three-point perspectives, but rather more similar to two-point perspectives drawn sideways—to a "vertical horizon," as it were. This simplification was possible because of the selection of symmetrical views from station points located on the center plane (corresponding to the section perspective cut line) of the project.

The arresting drama and spatial quality yielded by these unusual views should be self-evident. Looking up at the enormous and complex construction is almost daunting, and looking down from such a height is commanding, if vertiginous. Central Park South and the column at Columbus Circle are visible beyond the sloping glazed wall shown in the last drawing, along with a few of the work spaces of the firm whose headquarters will be housed in this truly New York–scale project.

New York, New York
Moshe Safdie & Associates
Section perspective
Black Prismacolor and ink on vellum drymounted to board (retrocolored)
12" × 10"
Seven days (1986)

(page 52)
Interior perspective (looking up)
Black Prismacolor on vellum drymounted to board (retrocolored)
12" × 10"
Eight days (1986)

(page 53)
Interior perspective (looking down)
Black Prismacolor on vellum drymounted to board (retrocolored)
12" × 10"
Eight days (1986)

3 Washington Projects

Pennsylvania Avenue Landscape and Lighting Proposal

These two drawings of Washington, D.C.'s Pennsylvania Avenue were commissioned to show the character of certain landscaping and lighting proposals at night as well as in the daytime. They are both color original wax-base pencil drawings on charcoal paper —beige for the daytime view and black for the night.

An available photograph was used to determine the layout of existing elements in both views. Salient lines were transferred from the photograph to the final drawing sheet by the use of white transfer paper for the night view, and graphite for the daytime.

This "blind transfer" technique is necessary with an opaque final drawing sheet or board, whereas simple tracing may be used with a translucent final such as vellum or film. The transfer process requires the firm use of a stylus, such as a ballpoint pen, directly on the photograph; since the stylus leaves indentations or even marks, the print should be considered dispensible.

In the case of the night-view transfer, the starkly white lines appearing on the final black sheet had to be reduced in intensity by the use of a kneaded eraser. The technique also has advantages, however: areas of transferred white were used intentionally to define headlights, street lights, and illuminated windows, and are much brighter than a white pencil is capable of producing on black paper.

There is some loss of impact resulting from the absence of color in this reproduction, notably the brilliant red tail lights of the cars on the right. As emitted chromatic illumination, the tail-lights provide by far the most intense color accent in the original night view, but are visible here only as a dim gray.

In the daytime view on the following page, the specificity of automobile models, makes, and even model years may be something of a distraction and should probably have been avoided. This kind of information can date a drawn image very quickly. See, for example, the reverse side of a ten-dollar bill, which depicts another Washington scene including the U.S. Treasury building. The engraving is quite precisely dated by the rather severely out-of-perspective drawing of the late 1920s sedan in the foreground.

Washington, D.C.
Sasaki Associates
Perspective view (night)
Prismacolor on black charcoal paper
8″ × 10″
Two days (1978)

(page 56)
Perspective view (day)
Prismacolor on Strathmore board
8″ × 10″
Three days (1978)

Washington Square Development

The drawings on the next pages describe a mixed-use downtown Washington development project as it would be seen at night as well as during the day. This day/night pairing of views differs from the previous project in that it shows a building rather than an avenue, and it employs some different media choices.

The drawings were made originally in black-and-white (for later retrocolor application) and were executed on a Strathmore illustration board for the day view, and on black 100 percent rag museum board for the night perspective. This is a typical board combination for other day/night pairs of drawings shown later in the book, as it is the most effective we have yet found for use with wax-base pencil.

The use of "scoring" to indicate mullions in large areas of glazing is apparent in the corresponding day and night locations. The daytime expression is a thin white line against a dark (penciled) background, and the nighttime expression is just the negative—a thin black line against a light (penciled) background. Black pencil can sometimes be used very sparingly for corrective purposes in night drawings, but it is easy to forget where it is located and accidently go over it with white, which produces a messy gray texture that is virtually impossible to repair.

This daytime view of a building with quite a bit of angular glass presents an opportunity to show a certain richness in the façade through careful indication of reflections. Notice, for example, the differences in reflectivity and transparency on the three major visible sides of the large octagonal "lantern" shown on the near corner. The center panel, which is viewed straight-on, is virtually transparent, while the two side panels, seen at raking angles, are shown reflecting the building face itself on the left and the sky to the right.

The compositional strategems used differ considerably in the day and night views. The latter makes use of the tried-and-true device of wet, reflective pavement, which provides an expanding and enriching dimension within the drawing. The daytime view relies compositionally on the dark existing building in shade at the left as well as its shadow across the foreground as framing elements. Observe the reflected image of the rounded corner of the same existing building in the sixth-floor glazing of the new building.

Washington, D.C.
Chloethiel Woodward Smith & Associates
(page 58)
Exterior perspective (night view)
White Prismacolor on black museum board
16" × 21"
Four days (1981)

(page 59)
Exterior perspective (day)
Black Prismacolor on Strathmore board
16" × 21"
Five days (1981)

Willard Hotel Rehabilitation Proposal

The particular challenge of this black-and-white drawing of a competitive proposal for the rehabilitation of a landmark Washington hotel was to suggest the character of the interior space, while conveying a precisely descriptive view of the exterior courtyard design. In attempting this, we made the interior dining space quite dark and with a fairly coarse texture, but took care not to lose all indication of the richly modeled plaster work in the ceiling.

The exterior scene, which includes a peek beyond to Pennsylvania Avenue, is dominated by curving walls with band glazing and by a radial series of white tubular trusses. It may be noted that mutual reflections of glazing bands are identical when a curved wall meets a straight one—that is, they both curve, as may be seen in the upper right portion of the picture. The distorted reflection of the planar wall bends in the curved wall, while the true reflection of the curved wall bends in the planar wall.

The rendering of the two stainless-steel elevators shown in the far right of the picture was aided by the addition of some miscellaneous objects (such as lipstick cases) as visual references. A little effort to understand the geometry of the cylindrical and spherical parts of the objects, and how they distort reflected images was very helpful in the realistic suggestion of the material and shape of the elevators. It may be of interest to refer also to the bridges sheathed in stainless steel in the Columbus Center project in the previous chapter.

Architectural perspectivists are frequently asked to include festive elements such as banners in their drawings. Although these are frequently major elements in the format, only occasionally have they received any design attention by the architect at the time of the drawing. That leaves this graphically important design task to the illustrator, who usually welcomes it if there is sufficient time to give it appropriate consideration.

Since graphic vagueness is usually inappropriate treatment for focal objects in the composition, I find it is helpful to assume some principle that can inform and relate to the design these otherwise random elements. In this illustration, I have chosen to use stylized letters on the series of hanging banners to spell out the name of the hotel.

Washington, D.C.
Arthur Cotton Moore Associates
Interior perspective
Black Prismacolor on vellum
14" × 17"
Five days (1978)

MetroCenter Development

This urban aerial drawing is a classic example of the delineator's problem of defining a project's limits when showing it within the context of a city. Sensitive and conscientious architects are likely to design structures of such scale and rhythm to fit easily into the existing urban fabric. This very sensitivity can make the delineator's task more challenging—particularly if a client wants to see his project stand out and be obviously identifiable. (See also the 499 Park Avenue project in the previous chapter.)

The two compositional devices used to address the problem of definition were those of selective contrast and, particularly, selective resolution. The three buildings composing the actual proposal are simply shown in greater detail and with generally greater contrast than are their existing surroundings. In fact, you may observe that the graphic resolution reduces progressively with distance from the project. The foreground—particularly the lower right quadrant—should have been drawn with lower resolution and contrast to be consistent with this compositional strategy.

Looking down at a building with a great deal of glazing is very different from viewing it at eye level. The lower viewpoint yields glazing of a generally light value because of sky reflection, particularly where the view is raking, whereas the aerial perspective shows predominantly dark ground reflections in the glass. Not entirely dark to be sure, as you will see on the left façade of the left building of the project.

It is almost always useful to construct first the image that would be seen reflected in a plane mirror of glazing (with no columns or spandrels), then add the matte parts of the architecture, taking care to double the reveal depth of windows as seen in reflection. You can observe the difference that varying depths of reveal make in the upper floors of the two nearer buildings of the project.

The issue of whether to include roof-mounted mechanical equipment obviously arises with some frequency in aerial drawings. Because the equipment is usually placed so that it will disappear from the eye-level view, and its precise location, size, and configuration are seldom known when a presentation drawing is made, we normally choose to delete roof "garbage" as we have done in this case. This choice has the incidental effect of helping to identify the project buildings, as the surrounding structures generally have more cluttered roofscapes.

Washington, D.C.
Skidmore, Owings & Merrill (Washington, D.C.)
Aerial perspective
Black Prismacolor on Strathmore board
13" × 18"
Five days (1981)

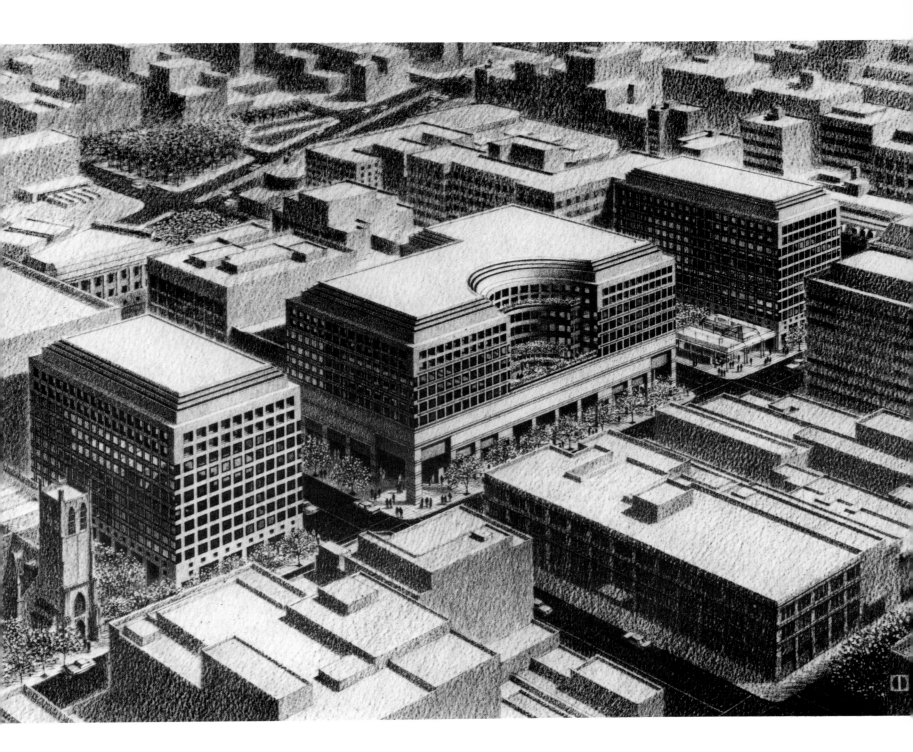

Vietnam Veterans Memorial (Competition)

In 1981, one of the most remarkable architectural competitions in many years was held for the design of a fitting memorial for Americans who gave their lives in the Vietnam war. Over fourteen hundred entries were received, including one designed by a group with which I was associated.

The winning entry was designed by Maya Ying Lin, then a twenty-one-year-old Yale undergraduate student. Her design, now familiar to everyone, was a shallow, V-shaped depression formed by two black granite retaining walls, upon which the names of some 57,000 individual American casualties were inscribed. The inclusion of individual names was a competition requirement. Since her original competition drawings describing the scheme were very abstract and legible only to professionals, there was an immediate need to communicate the nature of the design to the public. The drawings on the following pages are two of the three commissioned for that purpose. Because of severe schedule constraints, they were made quickly and at a small size, although the two summer views were drawn as color originals.

The two granite walls are oriented to align directly with the Washington Monument and the Lincoln Memorial, so it seemed appropriate to show these two general views relating to those familiar references. In introducing a seasonal variation, we intended to remind the viewer of the passage of time, and of the permanence of the memorial. The starkness of the white snow and black granite in the winter view seems particularly consistent with the abstract, minimalist character of the design. In the summer view, the figure with long black hair wearing a white blouse and pork-pie hat represents Maya Lin herself.

The earliest version of these drawings indicated a different detail at the top of the granite wall—one in which the stone projected several inches above grade. This detail was introduced by associates in response to technical requirements for maintenance and safety, and was *not* the original intention of the designer. The drawing showing this unacceptable detail was instrumental in the process of seeking and ultimately finding other means of solving those problems in a fashion more consistent with the original design. Here, the presentation drawing provided a catalyst for more effective and appropriate design, in addition to communicating that design to the public.

Washington, D.C.
P. S. Oles, Robert T. Gunn, et al.
Exterior perspective
Black Prismacolor on vellum with partial textural underlay
6½" × 11"
Two days (1981)

(page 66)
Maya Ying Lin
Exterior perspective (summer)
Prismacolor on Strathmore board
8½" × 11"
Two days (1981)

(page 67)
Maya Ying Lin
Exterior perspective (winter)
Black Prismacolor on Strathmore board
8½" × 11"
Two days (1981)

Washington Cathedral

This drawing was commissioned by the building committee of the Cathedral in order to show the building as it will appear when completed. In construction since 1907, the Cathedral had reached partial completion, as shown in the inset photograph, when the drawing was made. Since the financing of the building relies heavily on private contributions, this representation of the completed edifice was needed for fund-raising purposes. A limited edition of 250 signed lithographs was produced and presented to potential donors and church officials shortly after the drawing was completed in 1981.

The drawing required an extraordinary length of time to produce—almost seven months. This was, interestingly enough, approximately proportional to the unusually long construction time required for the building itself. Working drawings, including elevations, plans, and many horizontal sections, were used in addition to perspectives and photographs of the partially complete building to provide information upon which to base the meticulously constructed perspective.

We chose an early afternoon sun position providing raking shadows to indicate the depth and intricacy of the west façade. The dark upper sky and low clouds were shown to emphasize the verticality of the towers and lightness of the stone color. The shadow of the unseen trees to the right serves the compositional purpose of providing a darker, more substantial base for the drawing as well as suggesting the actual surroundings.

Interestingly, this particularly descriptive view of the building cannot be photographed—even after the building is completed—because of the location of major existing trees. This "drawing of the future" may continue to be used to describe the Washington Cathedral graphically even after its projected completion around the year 2000.

Washington, D.C.
Philip Hubert Frohman
Exterior perspective
Black Prismacolor on Strathmore board
32" × 26"
Twenty-four days (1981)

This photograph by the author shows the partially completed cathedral in 1981, at the time the drawing was executed.

Fairfax County Administrative Complex (Competition)

Drawings made for competition entry almost always have at least two implied requirements, execution speed and graphic impact. The following pair of competition drawings for this governmental building near Washington, D.C., offered no exception to that rule. Accordingly, we used as a base medium the dependable combination of vellum with a watercolor paper underlay throughout both formats.

Using a coarse, grainy-textured underlay increases drawing speed, which is clearly advantageous. Impact, power, or "drama" usually comes with simplicity, and tends to be antithetical to intricacy and detail. The underlay ensures that excessive detail will neither slow the drawing process nor detract from showing the overall conceptual idea—always crucial in a competitive exhibition context.

An absence of fine detail is also appropriate in describing a scheme that has not been resolved to the level of working drawings, as is the case here and in most competitions. It can be argued generally that the level of graphic resolution of a drawing should reflect the design resolution of the building it represents. For an example of extremely low drawing resolution showing a building early in its design phase, see the Miami World Trade Center project in chapter 5.

The plan of the building is not based upon a rectangular module, but rather upon a series of parallelograms. This leads to some rather interesting perceptual aberrations in both drawings. The eye is so accustomed to seeing forms with right angles that a photograph or drawing of any angle near 90 degrees will invariably be perceived as a precise right angle.

This perceptual phenomenon occurs when we view a photograph or drawing with a very wide angle perspective, which causes right angles, especially those at the edges of the format, to be seen as severely acute. Thus, when we see the sharp angles of the floors of this building, we may understandably assume that they represent right angles casually drawn. However, all the critical corners in these two drawings are within or near the limits of the standard 60 degree cone of vision, and thus are not distorted.

Fairfax County, Virginia
Cambridge Seven Associates (L. Bakanowski)
Exterior perspective (general view)
Black Prismacolor on vellum with textural underlay
7" × 14"
Three days (1982)

(page 72)
Exterior perspective (detail)
Black Prismacolor on vellum with textural underlay
7" × 14"
Three days (1982)

Naval Memorial Proposal

These eye-level views looking east and west on Pennsylvania Avenue depict a project relegated to the category of "alternative futures." The triumphal arch structure was proposed for the Naval Memorial, which has since been constructed in a very different form. The drawings are historical documents, however, permanently describing this particular design offering.

It is crucial, particularly in the case of a monumental project such as this, to show the relationship of the project to its important and familiar surroundings clearly. The importance of context is apparent in these drawings, since the proposed structure occupies no more than 10 percent of the format of either picture. The two views were necessary to show the relationship of the object (which is not orthogonal to the curbline) to an observer traveling either way on Pennsylvania Avenue.

Notice that resolution of the drawing is sharp near the vanishing point in the view toward the Capitol, while it is quite vague in the opposite direction. The view to the west is not only less important, but, because the view is juxtaposed with the arch in the drawing, detail could have proven distracting.

The Capitol building and the arch itself were drawn meticulously with a highly sharpened pencil under a magnifier, whereas most of the remainder of the format was produced more speedily. Tree foliage and foliage shadow—fairly important in both views —were drawn with a very dull point since it was not possible to use an underlay with the thick illustration board. The foreground shadows in the view looking east suggest the presence of trees immediately behind the viewer, even though none is visible in the picture.

The group of figures shown in the midground of the west view is an example of a scale device used to good advantage. The figures are in shadow, which removes all detail save for silhouette (therefore reducing their "social distraction"), and they are situated near enough the viewer to communicate the sense that this is indeed a precisely eye-level view, since the horizon occurs at their eye level.

Washington, D.C.
Conklin & Rossant, Architects
(page 74)
Exterior perspective (east view)
Black Prismacolor on Strathmore board (retrocolored)
9″ × 13″
Four days (1982)

(page 75)
Exterior perspective (west view)
Black Prismacolor on Strathmore board (retrocolored)
9″ × 13″
Four days (1982)

Potomac Park Point Building Proposal

This high-tech building design was the initial part of an extensive proposal for a corporate residential development on several hundred wooded acres near Dulles Airport. The building itself was designed to serve as a reception and demonstration center, with an observation tower from which the entire expanse of the development could be seen.

The general configuration of the plan is semicircular, with glazed, planar-faced segments along the convex side defined by the exposed roof trusses fanning from a central point. It is a particularly difficult form to show adequately in a single drawing, and can be shown effectively from very few eye-level viewpoints. Fortunately, a model was available and provided an indispensable aid in the selection of a station point. I made a sketch from what seemed to be the best single station point, then the angle and proportional distance to my eyes were measured, recorded, and used in constructing the final drawing.

The choice of lighting angle was virtually as crucial to the drawing as was the selection of station point. Since we see the north side of the building, it is shown in shade with early morning light streaming in from the east. That decision suggested a sky graded from light to dark at the right, which formed a superb value foil for the observation tower, which would be brilliantly illuminated on its east face by the morning sunlight.

The principal material of the building is semireflective white metal panels, similar to those used in the MIT Arts and Media Technology building project. As with that building, it was difficult to indicate clearly the partially reflective nature of the surface— particularly in a normal view toward the shade side. In the retrocolored version of this drawing, color provided additional helpful cues by allowing the green tint of diffusely reflected trees to suggest the slickness of the panels.

Loudoun County, Virginia
VVKR Inc.
Exterior perspective
Black Prismacolor on vellum with textural underlay (retrocolored)
12″ × 17″
Six days (1986)

U.S. Holocaust Memorial Museum

This night view describes a proposed structure to house the exhibitions and artifacts commemorating the systematic extinction of Jews attempted by the Nazi regime during the Second World War. The daytime view shown in the inset is an earlier version of the same building shown from the identical station point, which is located on 15th Street near the Mall in Washington, D.C.

The two views are part of a series showing paired viewpoints looking east and west, developed during the process of design as an aid to that process. The proposed building is sited between the auditor's building on the left side and the federal mint on the right. This location makes the two facades parallel to 14th and 15th streets very important since the long façades on the north and south cannot be seen from any appreciable distance.

The night view was drawn on black 100 percent rag museum board with white wax-base pencil, as is the case for most night drawings shown in this book. The transfer from the constructed layout was made with white Saral paper; the resulting white lines were then selectively minimized with an X-acto knife and a kneaded eraser. A diagonal lighting composition resulted from the natural circumstances of the building's situation in the view. The bright area in the lower right part of the picture is caused by light spill from the illuminated center of the building, and the hazy whitish sky in the upper left quadrant suggests the glow from the nearby Washington Monument and the more distant Capitol building.

The highlighted bronze sculpture in the center of the façade is intended to suggest a group of prisoners behind barbed wire. An element as small as wire had obviously to be exaggerated for visibility, and this was accomplished graphically through the use of scoring. I designed this sculpture for inclusion in the drawing only, at the client's request, in the same way that I designed the banners shown in the Willard Hotel project. The final sculpture, which will undoubtedly be commissioned, may bear little resemblance to the image shown here.

As a 1987 postscript, the building itself will bear little resemblance to the image shown here. The design commission was later transferred to another architect, for whom we also provided the drawings, but the project was finished too late to be included in this book.

Washington, D.C.
Notter, Finegold & Alexander
Exterior perspective (night view)
White Prismacolor on black museum board
11" × 17"
Four days (1985)

This drawing by the author shows a daytime view of an earlier design of the museum.

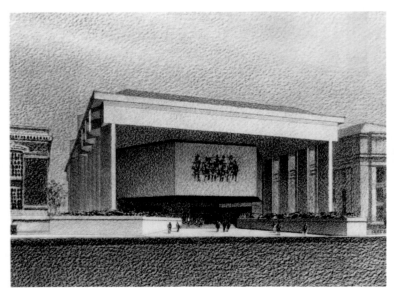

4 Texas Projects

Dallas Centre Development

This drawing of the first of three office towers for the Dallas Centre Development proved to be one of the most challenging and, I believe, most successful we have undertaken to date.

The challenges mainly involved predicting the mutual inter-reflections in the glazing of the two principal façades. The inter-reflections were painstakingly constructed, then verified through observation of specially prepared Plexiglas mock-ups. The moiré patterns in the reflections of the facing buildings were discovered only after the value study was completed. Unfortunately, those patterns, which require the existence of both façades, can never be verified because the second tower will not be built.

However, we knew at the outset that this particular view could never be replicated by photograph anyway, because the station-point location was chosen to be well inside an existing building opposite the new project. This use of an implied station point is typical in a dense urban center, when a horizontal (two-point) eye-level perspective drawing is used to describe a tall building. A horizontal view (as distinct from a vertical, or three-point, perspective) requires a substantial amount of distance between the viewer and the drawn object to avoid undue distortion. Sometimes, as in this case, that distance requires the temporary removal or finessing of existing buildings or other urban furniture. In this respect, the architectural perspectivist has a definite advantage over the architectural photographer.

Although the general character of the drawing is photographic, another liberty not available to the photographer is the use of a clarifying device I refer to as *aura*. See, for example, the light haze on the left side of the tower. The main function of aura (a technique used extensively by Hugh Ferriss) is to separate planes visually that are actually separated by distance—particularly when those planes are close to each other in value. In this drawing it was important that the dark building on the left not be perceived as part of the form of the designed tower.

Dallas, Texas
I. M. Pei & Partners (H. Cobb)
Exterior perspective
Black Prismacolor on vellum drymounted to board
22" × 15"
Nine days (1977)

Commercial Bank Tower Proposal

This drawing was completed several months after the Dallas tower project. Although similar in some respects, it differs from the earlier drawing in several ways. The viewpoint, for example, was selected to show the building from a physically accessible rather than an implied position. As a result, we used existing buildings as a compositional frame for the proposed tower. We took advantage of the open corner of the existing building in the left foreground to show the edge of the proposed project; the low façade would otherwise have seemed to be of indeterminate if not infinite length. This overlapped "peek-a-boo" arrangement seems to relate the existing and proposed buildings to one another in an especially effective way.

Another dissimilarity from the earlier drawing is in the use of foreground figures and cars, a scale-giving strategy that is not possible when an implied station point is used. The shadow cast by the existing building on the right conveniently allowed us to suppress various details of the foreground elements, and serves to incorporate them into the dark, prosceniumlike frame.

That darkness ends on the left side halfway up the picture, where the existing building wall receives direct sunlight. Notice that the edge of the shadow is shown as quite soft. This was done because the shadow is cast from the top of the building to the right, which is a considerable distance away. The hardness of a shadow edge depends on its distance from the casting edge.

The geometry of forms at the top of the projected building is potentially misleading because the drawing substantially exceeds the 60 degree cone of vision of a standard perspective drawing. This alteration of the normal cone of vision is a frequent result of selecting an actual rather than an implied urban station point. However, in a densely developed city center, it is usually difficult to find an actual station point sufficiently distant from the project to permit a clear view of the project within the normal vision cone. The 45 degree chamfer on the left element of the tower may look more like a right angle to an observer, particularly to one who is unfamiliar with the plan design of the scheme. The actual right angle between the two façades of the right-hand element tends to look like a severely acute angle, a condition that is all too typical in the conventional representation of orthogonal towers.

Reflection plays a much less important role in this drawing than in the preceding one. Reflection is useful, however, in communicating the geometry of the modified Chicago window with side lights canted at 45 degrees in plan. The amount of light reflected by the several panes varies substantially because of the great difference in glazing angle. Since the angle of reveal is doubled by its reflection, the apparent depth and vigor of the low façade is enhanced by the reflections shown in the glazing.

Fort Worth, Texas
I. M. Pei & Partners (H. Cobb)
Exterior perspective
Black Prismacolor on vellum (retrocolored)
20" × 12½"
Seven days (1977)

82

ARAMCO Tower Proposal

This project was undertaken some three years after the previous two Texas towers, and is located adjacent to yet another Pei skyscraper design of earlier vintage. The Texas Commerce Tower, visible in the right side of this picture, is a 1977 project, our drawing of which is shown on this page as an inset.

The ARAMCO drawing offers a good illlustration of the dependable "light building/dark sky" value strategy in which the sunlit building face is lighter than the mid-value sky, and the shade side is darker than sky value. This works to particular advantage here to celebrate the stepped setback on each of the two visible façades, showing one as the negative of the other in terms of value. The lower part of the building is also stepped, and can be seen through the columns of the existing theater arcade on the left. This aspect of the proposal's design, similar to that in the previous drawing, aids the visual integration of the existing and proposed structures.

The building façade design, like many to follow it in the next decade, is composed of coplanar materials of differing darkness in a carefully studied two-dimensional pattern. The darker stone facing forms a large square module (consistent with the scale of the stepped corners) that contains a smaller, window-scaled module defined by lighter material. In order to preserve value constancy from the sunlit to the shade side of the tower, some care had to be taken with these relative values. You may notice that the level of module detail resolution diminishes with height, although building edge contours remain sharp to emphasize the simplicity and power of the stepped form against the sky.

Since the building was not juxtaposed with other towers when the drawing was begun, reflections were not a major illustration consideration. The absence of cloud configuration in the smoothly graded sky further simplifies the character of the drawn façades. To see the effects of a clouded sky on glazed towers, turn to the drawing of Fountain Place on pages 88 and 89.

Houston, Texas
I. M. Pei & Partners (H. Fredenburgh)
Exterior perspective
Black Prismacolor on vellum
20" × 10"
Four days (1980)

This 1977 drawing by the author shows the adjacent Texas Commerce Tower (also by I. M. Pei) from the arcade pictured in the later drawing.

Atlantic Richfield Tower

Continuing the Texas tower series, this 1978 drawing of I. M. Pei's design for a major oil company's headquarters shows its situation in downtown Dallas. Its most specific and memorable neighbor, certainly from a pedestrian's viewpoint, would be the small spiral chapel dominating a triangular site called Thanksgiving Square. The chapel is shown here in shadow from an adjacent building, so it is impossible to define it by usual means for directly sunlit objects. Thus, the chapel is shaded lighter toward the edges, which is typical for cylindrical objects illuminated only by diffuse sky light. In my best retrospective judgment, I believe that it is shown here somewhat lighter than would be possible for it to appear in this context without some internal illumination and translucent walls.

The existing surrounding buildings provide a convenient frame for the proposed tower. The reflected image of one building can be seen in the right-hand façade of the building, and provides an opportunity for a value counterchange from light building against dark sky, at the top of the right side, to its reverse at the lower floors. The rendering shows the surrounding buildings as slightly simplified, and at a somewhat lower resolution than the proposed tower. This was done for compositional coherence as well as to increase drawing speed and efficiency.

It should be noted that there is a certain amount of ambiguity in the skyline form, although it is not possible to correct such ambiguity in this kind of drawing, with a relatively low station point. Unlike the Dallas Centre design, one façade of this rhombus-shaped building plan ends at a higher elevation than the other. It might appear that the higher side is only one or two feet thick, when actually the edge seen from this viewpoint is simply the acute vertex of the triangular floor plan of the several uppermost floors.

A minor technical and compositional problem carried by this stepladder, or higher than eye-level, viewpoint is the visible vanishing point on the right side of the picture. Without resorting to such means as selective de-resolution, it is difficult to keep the viewer's eye from being constantly attracted to the pinhole at the end of the mile-long street. In eye-level drawings, a visible vanishing point can frequently be made to appear as the tiny head of a distant person, but even in Texas it is difficult to imagine a five-story-tall scale figure.

Dallas, Texas
I. M. Pei & Partners (H. Cobb)
Exterior view
Black Prismacolor on Strathmore board
20" × 15"
Eight days (1978)

Fountain Place Development

Drawing a building that is composed almost entirely of reflective surfaces can be something of a challenge. The first and most important element required for an eye-level view of such a structure is an active and varied sky, so that various planes can reflect either dark or light areas of the sky, and can thus be distinguished from one another. Vigorous cloud forms offer further opportunity to remind the viewer that the building surfaces are reflective, not matte. (See also the Austral project in chapter 6.)

Those invented clouds became a compositional element, as did the areas of light and dark reflected in the various building surfaces. Because of the graphic complexity of their interaction, we undertook a careful value study of the various elements in order to obtain a preview of the drawing. Notice how critical intersections and corners are almost invariably defined by the relative foils of light and dark. Adjacent building reflections were modified slightly to aid in the definition of arrises and corners.

Parallel planes such as the sloping ones visible at the top and center of the building—shown here as very dark—must be treated similarly since they reflect the same part of the sky. Surprisingly, owing to the unusual geometry of the building, the large dark triangle at the building center is not seen reflected in the vertical wall to the right. This allows the large, clean, and powerfully simple trapezoid of building surface to reflect an imagined very light part of the sky to the left, forming the dramatic center to this composition of architectural geometrics. Mullions also help, in a subtle way, to define the orientation and relative positioning of the various intersecting planes.

The architectural elements and ground clutter have been simplified and minimized here in order to allow the exuberant geometry of the designed form to have full sway in the picture. As a purely abstract form, the building stands to benefit from concentration on the architectonic aspect of its existence, and that is what this drawing strives to celebrate.

Dallas, Texas
I. M. Pei & Partners (H. Cobb)
Exterior perspective
Black Prismacolor on Strathmore board (retrocolored)
18" × 11"
Seven days (1982)

This 1986 photograph by the author shows the first of two identical buildings that composed the original project.

Dallas Convention Center Addition

As in most drawings that show an addition to an existing structure, this one includes a portion of the existing convention center, shown at the left of the roadway median. That portion was chosen carefully to provide identity but not overwhelm the new addition, which is of course the main subject of the drawing. The trees along the median offer a convenient divider between existing and new structures, making it compositionally feasible to crop the drawing at the treeline should it become useful to show the drawing of the addition alone.

The drawing was executed on vellum with textural underlay of 140 pound D'Arches watercolor paper, used throughout almost the entire format as well. A great deal of care was taken to vary the texture from rough (foliage and tree shadows) to smooth (building faces, glazing) with the underlay in place. Signs and automobiles were drawn without the underlay—or, more precisely, with a smooth card interposed between the vellum and the watercolor paper. This method allowed us to change modes quickly from rough to smooth without having to remove the underlay sheet.

Tree and soffit reflections in the narrow glazed bands provide virtually the only cue to the fact that the bands are indeed windows. The same is true of the shadow reflection at the link between the two buildings. That diagonal shadow poses something of a perceptual ambiguity, since it so nearly coincides with the line of the parapet on the shade side of the addition. We tried to avoid a perfect alignment within the constraints of a believable sun angle for this specific site and season.

To be entirely consistent with the sun placement assumed for the drawing, the sky should have been made slightly lighter toward the right side, although that would not have helped the value composition. For an example of a photograph showing the substantial gradation of a late afternoon sky, see the MGF Center drawing on pages 95 and 96.

The dependable device of aura again came to the rescue in a rendering of the right-hand bay of the addition. It was imperative to show that the building was open on the first floor, but the foliage beyond the soffit was unfortunately the same value as the underside of the building in shade. The discreet use of aura along the soffit edge seemed to be the only available solution within the constraints of a black-and-white picture. Naturally, depicting the green foliage beyond a warm-hued building would have solved the problem neatly.

Dallas, Texas
Omniplan Architects
Exterior perspective
Black Prismacolor on vellum with partial textural underlay
10½" × 21"
Six days (1982)

Houston Design Center

This drawing illustrates admirably the efficacy of the section perspective and its capacity to show most or all of the important spatial relationships of an internally complex building. No conventional perspective view, interior or exterior, could carry quite so much information in one image without resorting to schematic means.

Selecting the correct viewpoint (and corresponding vanishing point) was crucial to the effectiveness of the illustration, because of the complexity and potential confusion of elements in the public circulation spaces, shown here in high resolution and contrast. The standard 60 degree cone of vision rule of perspective (i.e., that objects located outside the cone of vision will appear distorted) predicates using a viewpoint near the center of a drawing such as this one. We chose to establish the station point at the eye level of a person standing on the third level. This placement arrayed the series of stairways and escalators in a pattern mostly receding from the viewpoint, thereby clarifying their arrangement visually.

Since the proprietary areas to either side of the public circulation spaces were by nature unprogrammed (the space will be leased to various design manufacturers and distributers), we agreed with the architect's desire to show them as intentionally vague, and unrepresentationally light, to serve as a foil for the higher contrast public circulation spaces. In the retrocolor version of this drawing, the public/proprietary distinction has been heightened by the introduction of warm and cool tints, respectively, to the two zones.

The poché (that is, filled or hatched) value used in this section perspective is white rather than the more usual black (see the Portland Museum and Columbus Center drawings in the first two chapters). The reasons for using white are to lighten the drawing by allowing paper or "air" into its interior and to provide a better foil between the dark center portions of the drawing and the floor structure. Thin ink lines were used here as a poché edge, whereas in the case of a solid black poché, the area between the lines is filled by ink to provide a nonsmudging, sharp-edged absolute black that distinguishes the section plane clearly from the rest of the drawing.

Houston, Texas
Cambridge Seven Associates (C. Redmon)
Section perspective
Black Prismacolor and ink on Strathmore board
27" × 40"
Seven days (1981)

MGF Center Development Proposal

These two drawings describe a wonderfully ambitious building proposal for my home town of Midland, Texas, during the oil boom of the early 1980s. This sixty-story mixed-use tower would have dwarfed the existing office buildings of the town (which is nicknamed "Tall City" by local boosters), and the photomontage was assembled to show this relationship. The photograph was taken from the roof of a ten-story building, so the horizon intersects every building visible in the picture at its tenth floor. Notice the palpable brightening of the sky toward the west, or right-hand side, of this late afternoon photograph.

The eye-level view was executed unintentionally in two stages. The lower two-fifths of the final format were drawn as a complete picture showing only the street-level features, the lower hotel element, and the beginning of the office floors. We found that clients (particularly in Texas) want to see the *tops* of their buildings, so an extension of the original drawing was commissioned. The new drawing required us to match the original board precisely—especially in thickness—and to mount the old and new pieces to a rigid backing board. Despite utmost care, a fine but unavoidable joint is visible between the first and second phases of the drawing.

Extension of an existing drawing to this degree carried a few surprises. First, the elongation of the tower placed the top drastically out of the 60 degree cone of vision, resulting in a strange geometry at the termination of the building, similar to the Fort Worth tower shown earlier in this section. The second effect of the graft was the extreme darkening of the sky and lightening of the building at the top. Since the rate of gradation for both sky and building had been established in the original drawing, there was nothing to do but continue them to their natural conclusions. The result was an extreme contrast between the sunlit building face and surrounding sky—virtually white and black, respectively. In the perennial trade-off, information about the building is lost (specifically, spandrel detail), but brute graphic power and a heightened sense of drama are gained.

Another unusual feature of the drawing involves the tapered shape of the tower shaft. In a two-point perspective depiction of an ordinary vertical tower, this elongation of the tower—an extreme violation of the normal vision cone—would make the building look as if it were physically diverging toward the top. In this case, however, the actual convergence point of the sloping tower becomes an implied vertical vanishing point and reduces the impression of distortion.

Midland, Texas
I. M. Pei & Partners (H. Fredenburgh)
Exterior perspective (photomontage)
Prismacolor on Strathmore board
24" × 24"
Three days (1982)
(Photograph © Nathaniel Lieberman.)

(page 96)
Exterior perspective
Black Prismacolor on Strathmore board (retrocolored)
14" × 18"
Seven days (1982)
40" × 18"
Five days (1982)

CityPlace Development

These two finished drawings are part of a series of illustrations commissioned to describe this extensive corporate complex of headquarters, offices, and condominiums located astride a major freeway serving Dallas. A pair of views was considered necessary to show the relationship of the towers to each other and to the freeway, as well as to give a sense of the complex as entered from adjacent neighborhoods. The centers of vision of the two perspectives are therefore approximately perpendicular to each other.

The first of the two drawings on the following pages (showing both towers) posed a compositional difficulty that I call the "goalpost effect." To offset the almost unrelieved symmetry of the design, an off-center station point was selected that resulted in each of the two towers being shown, in effect, from differing viewpoints. Add to that the result of raking sunlight, which yields two façades of greatly differing overall values (because of the sawtoothed floor-plan design), and the off-center placement of the two towers in the format, and the composition becomes acceptably interesting.

This first view also allowed us to include an important foreground element—one of three bridges connecting the two halves of the project—and a view of the towers of Dallas in the distance. The tower locations were carefully determined by plotting sightlines on a city map, although they were finally shifted slightly for visibility. The second view was much less challenging compositionally, and the result is simpler and perhaps stronger than the first. The second tower is actually shown in this view, although it may not be immediately obvious.

In an unusual technical departure, I decided to mix media in these drawings. For speed, the sky and glazed areas of both drawings were toned not with pencil, but airbrush. This attempted shortcut did prove somewhat faster, but produced a sky value that, despite utmost care and patience, showed certain value and gradation irregularities that were impossible to tune out. Airbrush seems to be, for most practical purposes, a virtually untunable and most unforgiving medium. Since the drawings were retrocolored, the subsequent application of color allowed some tuning in of tone and texture.

Dallas, Texas
Araldo Cossutta & Associates
(page 98)
Exterior perspective (south view)
Black Prismacolor and airbrush on Strathmore board (retrocolored)
14" × 19"
Eight days (1984)

(page 99)
Exterior perspective (east view)
Black Prismacolor and airbrush on Strathmore board (retrocolored)
14" × 14"
Seven days (1984)

RepublicBank Tower Proposal

In preparing this drawing, which shows the lobby space for a tower design submitted as a competitive proposal, we were offered the good opportunity to work in an office with perhaps the most advanced computer-aided design system in the country. This view was one of two executed in a short time, both of which were made with the help of computer-generated layouts produced by the in-house computer system and staff.

The most remarkable component of the visualization system was an Evans and Sutherland PS-300 real-time interactive display. This marvelous machine allowed even an uninitiated person using a simple console to "fly" through a wireframe representation of the projected space. It quickly became easy to travel in real time (at an actual selected pace) from one part of the building to the other, to look left or right, up or down, and change the width of view at will. With a little skill in twirling two knobs at once, one could even move up a wireframe escalator, observing the changing three-point perspective view much as a photographer might do when looking for the perfect spot from which to take a picture.

When the perfect station point is located, one simply calls for a paper plot of the perspective array, and that can be used as an underlayout for the hand-drawn perspective. The inset image shows the plotted view used for this drawing. Although the hidden lines (representing edges not visible in the actual object) in this wireframe view have not been removed, the lines usually create little or no problem for the designer or delineator.

In fact, if the information is not too dense or ambiguously overlapping, visible "hidden lines" may be frequently useful to both designer and delineator. Perhaps a good compromise between the wishes of the computer technicians (who always want to remove the hidden lines) and the designers is to have a system of hidden-line suppression, with line visibility decreasing with distance from the viewer.

The drawing itself was produced quickly because of the schedule constraints of the competition. A coarse underlay was used with vellum, which produced a resolution level that seemed approximately consistent with the level of design precision at that point, although a bit more time could have been put to good use. The drawings were quickly photographed on mural paper, mounted on Gatorboard and retrocolored in Massachusetts, then shipped to Chicago in time for submission.

Dallas, Texas
Skidmore, Owings & Merrill (Chicago)
Interior perspective
Black Prismacolor on vellum with textural underlay (retrocolored)
18" × 15"
Three days (1984)

A print of this computer-generated wireframe perspective served as the base layout for the final drawing.

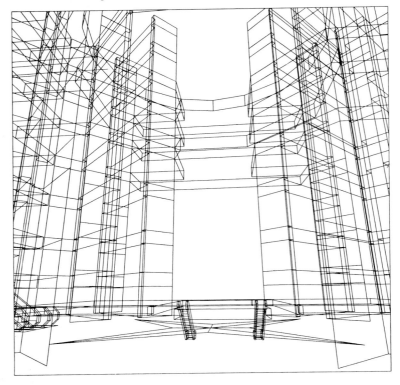

Dallas Symphony Hall

Dallas has long been one of the most construction-intensive cities of the American Sunbelt. A continuing municipal interest in the arts has led to the planning of a fine-arts precinct in which the project will be sited. Funding for the building was raised by a locally supported bond issue, which relied in part on these drawings to communicate the architect's intentions to the public.

The drawings of the lobby interior involved extensive study by means of computer-generated graphics, which were provided by Computervision, Inc., of Bedford, Massachusetts. Many dozens of perspective views led to the selection of this one as the most descriptive single view of all. An early evening lighting context was our final choice for two reasons: the building would frequently be in use during the twilight hours; and early evening light allowed greater subtlety in the rendering of interior form than would be possible with a very bright daytime sky visible through the large window and skylight openings. For instance, the two lighted onyx fixtures would be more difficult to illustrate in a daytime interior view.

The pair of exterior drawings on the next pages show from the same station point the character of the building in daylight and at night. These drawings were made from the same layout, with the night view executed on an orthogonally-textured charcoal paper, which explains the particular texture of this rendering. I usually prefer a random texture, which generates a coarseness that seems to be more a part of the represented three-dimensional world than of the two-dimensional world of the picture plane.

The daytime view was rendered with black Prismacolor pencil on Strathmore illustration board, a standard combination for our work. Naturally, it is possible to indicate a great deal more information about the exterior of the building in a daytime view, such as the highlighted glazed skylights. The varying angles of the building can also be shown with much greater subtlety than is possible at night. Following Lambert's law, incident sunlight produces varying luminance on the differently oriented stone surfaces of the building, and these slight shifts are carefully indicated through changing values in the daytime view.

Dallas, Texas
I. M. Pei & Partners (I. M. Pei)
Interior perspective
Black Prismacolor on vellum drymounted to board
12″ × 18½″
Ten days (1985)

(page 104)
Exterior perspective (day view)
Black Prismacolor on Strathmore board
13″ × 20″
Eight days (1982)

(page 105)
Exterior perspective (night view)
White Prismacolor on black charcoal paper
13″ × 20″
Seven days (1982)

5 Other United States Projects

Pacific Center Development Proposal

This representation of an early Kohn Pedersen Fox design is one of the more graphic, or two-dimensional, compositions that we have yet produced. This graphic quality resulted in part from our decision to locate the viewpoint on a center of vision placed between the two towers, which yielded a straight-on, or effectively one-point, perspective view. The picture plane is consequently parallel to the 45 degree chamfered walls of both towers, yielding this graphically simplified array of forms. Adding the abstract detail of the existing tower to the left and the absence of scale-defining foreground elements, the remaining pictorial task became one of shifting croplines to achieve a pleasing composition of virtually schematic graphic elements.

The drawing was executed on vellum drymounted on illustration board, an ideal combination for this precise high-resolution rendition of form. Note that the three major visible planes of the towers are shown in shade, raking sunlight, and direct sunlight, reading from left to right. This combination generally offers the greatest value distinction and, therefore, definition possible among triple sets of visible nonreflective, or composite, surfaces.

Notice also that in this typical glazing-spandrel value relationship the windows on the sunlit side of the right tower are darker than the spandrel, and the reverse is true on the shade side. This can leave the window and spandrel a bit close in value for the raked plane between, but because of the relatively dark sky in this picture we decided to allow the glass to be seen as slightly darker than usual. In this drawing, both the glazing and the spandrels are graded from lighter near the horizon to darker toward the tops of the towers.

There is a certain amount of interest in this fairly aescetic rendering of a severe subject, provided in the local value gradations (caused by "light bounce" from the stepped balconies) and also in the interreflections in the glazing bands of the first few floors between the two towers. The single foreground car on the entrance ramp is intended to suggest the presence of the freeway, which has been depressed to minimize traffic noise and specifically to disappear from sight in views such as this.

Los Angeles, California
Kohn Pedersen Fox Associates
Exterior perspective
Black Prismacolor on vellum drymounted to board
18½" × 16½"
Six days (1978)

Johnson & Johnson Headquarters

The vignette format is ideally suited to partial or detail views of extensive projects such as this corporate headquarters complex. In the pair of drawings shown on these pages, the vignette was chosen also for its softness (to contrast with a geometrically assertive building) and for the advantage it offers in drawing speed.

This format type, which also may be seen in the New York Public Library and RepublicBank drawings, has specific compositional requirements, including the diminution of contrast as well as resolution toward the edges of the picture. For this reason the sky value is inverted from the normal lighter-at-the-horizon gradation that is the rule for clear days. The darker low sky additionally facilitates the skyline definition of the white buildings.

Textural distinction between smooth building surfaces and coarse foliage was aided by the selective use of a watercolor paper underlay beneath the tree forms and their shadows. The "negative pencil," or sharpened electric eraser, was most useful for quick removal of small areas of tone in trees and shadows to suggest sunlit leaves and dappled patterns of shade.

The window bands and larger areas of corner glass provided one of the main areas of challenge and opportunity in these drawings. Re-entrant or interior corner glazing lends itself naturally to the illustration of the reflective/transparent quality of glass through the simple geometric construction of the mutual reflections. Notice that the reflection of an adjacent surface in the glazing is usually shown as slightly darker than the image of the surface itself. In other areas the transparency of glazing is more apparent —for example, in the corner glazing of the tower and the larger glass areas of the low-rise building, as shown on page 110. The monochromatic images shown here subsequently served as originals for photographically enlarged retrocolored prints to be used for presentation.

New Brunswick, New Jersey
I. M. Pei & Partners (H. Cobb)
Exterior perspective
Black Prismacolor on laminated vellum (retrocolored)
15" × 20"
Five days (1978)

(page 110)
Exterior perspective
Black Prismacolor on laminated vellum (retrocolored)
15" × 20"
Five days (1978)

Southeast Bell Headquarters Proposal (Competition)

The drawings on the following two pages were prepared for a competition submission, and as is usual for competitions, there were severe schedule constraints. We drew the images quite small for the sake of speed, and subsequently enlarged them photographically with paper prints mounted to the final submission boards.

The interior view shows the courtyard of the torus-shaped main structure from a viewpoint far enough inside the building to give some sense of looking out. The design makes it possible to see not only the opposite side of the "doughnut," but farther to the water beyond, allowing us to look from inside to outside to in to out again. The foreground figures, purposely vague in detail, are edge-lighted to suggest that the most intense light emanates from outside the window.

The glass wall on the left, which we view at an extremely raked angle, shows a substantial reflection of the diagonal shadow on the concrete stair element. The glass would be virtually transparent in the zone reflecting the dark shadow, and in effect opaque because of veiling lightness in zones that reflect sunlit concrete or especially sky. We have not shown this phenomenon as strongly here as a photograph would, but have adopted a compromise affording greater transparency than the glazing would actually provide. Many designing architects tend to forget that glass viewed at a sharply raking angle loses almost all of its transparency because of increased reflectivity, particularly when viewed from the exterior side.

Execution speed was my overriding concern again in the production of the two required exterior views showing the phasing of construction. Rather than redraw nearly all of the phase-one view for phase two, I decided to make only opaque paper "patches" showing future building additions, and photograph these in place over the original first-phase drawing. The two patches were tacked face side up under a Plexiglas cover that was hinged at the top of the board of the original base drawing, allowing the second-phase option to be flipped in or out easily.

The photograph providing the copy for the second-phase image presented here was taken through its Plexiglas cover. As you can see, photographing through a single thickness of clean Plexiglas causes no appreciable deterioration of an image; both phases share the same sharpness and clarity. The gain in schedule time purchased by this shortcut was used to provide more precisely resolved finished drawings than would otherwise have been possible.

Nashville, Tennessee
The Architects Collaborative (J. Harkness)
(page 112)
Interior perspective
Black Prismacolor on vellum drymounted to board
8" × 10"
Four days (1980)

(page 113)
Aerial perspective (phase one)
Black Prismacolor on vellum drymounted to board
9" × 15"
Four days (1980)

(page 113)
Aerial perspective (phase two)
Black Prismacolor on opaque paper mounted to Plexiglas overlay
9" × 15"
Two days (1980)

Miami World Trade Center

This tower perspective is included here as an example of perhaps the least detailed, lowest resolution drawing we have provided for final public presentation. Although increased drawing speed is obviously gained by this type of presentation, neither the schedule nor the budget was the operative constraint in this case. Rather, it was the architect's wish to achieve high impact and graphic drama, somewhat in the tradition of Hugh Ferriss.

Ferriss images are known for their power, achieved through the inspired application of the entire range of possible values, and not especially for their precision or completeness of information. Information, it could be argued, may generally be inversely proportional to inspiration. This is an equation that, I am sure, has notable exceptions, but it provided a major guideline for this particular drawing.

There are several intentional differences between this drawing and what would be a quintessential Ferriss version of it. To begin with, Ferriss would probably make use of a much more linear, visible pencil stroke to establish sky values, instead of allowing only the paper texture to determine the nondirectional grain of the sky. Doubtless he would make much greater use of aura, particularly between the dark foreground building to the left and the low element of the tower. Ferriss might even have made values darker toward the corners of the format, and I would not be surprised to see a silhouetted construction crane included somewhere in the picture. The foreground has been uncluttered and schematized even more drastically than in the Fountain Place drawing shown in chapter 4. To increase even further the level of abstraction and add a bit to the perceived height of the tower, I've introduced a certain amount of reflectivity into the foreground. This has the effect, I believe, of dematerializing, or suppressing, the surroundings and contributing to the sense of the building as a discrete object, or even a carefully designed "product." Innocent of scale or specific context, this image may be somewhat less true to photographic reality than most drawings are in this book, but the equation is balanced in my judgment by a gain in simple dramatic power.

Miami, Florida
I. M. Pei & Partners (H. Fredenburgh)
Exterior perspective
Black Prismacolor on vellum with textural underlay
17" × 12½"
Three days (1980)

114

Cleveland Clinic

For this straightfoward drawing of a deceptively simple building, the viewpoint selection, value arrangement, and format composition were all considered with particular care. We agreed early in the drawing process that the viewpoint should be from eye level. With that as a given, it became immediately obvious that the building should be seen from some three-quarter view in order to communicate an idea of its depth. A straight-on one-point perspective would yield little more information than an elevation drawing would. The final viewpoint selection was made to catch the left-hand corner of the clinic between the tall chimney and roof of the adjacent church. (See the Fort Worth tower drawing in chapter 4 for a similar existing/proposed relationship).

The sky value shows the classic and predictable clear-day gradation toward a lighter horizon and a lighter sun side, shown on the right side of the picture. This arrangement provides adequate foil for this fairly dark building but can be a problem with lighter buildings whose skylines tend to disappear along both the sunlit and shade sides. The nonglazing material of this building is graded from a lighter base to a darker skyline mainly because of "ground bounce," or light reflected from the surrounding ground plane. The mirror glazing, although much lighter, follows the same direction of gradation because of the sky it is reflecting.

The façade reflection of an unseen adjacent building is particularly important to this drawing, helping to establish the sense of glazing reflectivity and the context in which the clinic is situated. In the original color version of the drawing, the cool shade side of the reflected building is somewhat more well-defined against the warm sunlit façade of the clinic than in this duotone reproduction.

Cleveland, Ohio
Cesar Pelli & Associates
Exterior perspective
Prismacolor on Strathmore board
13″ × 18″
Four days (1981)

Miami Center Development

This drawing of an extensive development for downtown Miami would have required a substantial amount of time to construct a perspective layout, had it not been for the existence of a large, highly detailed, and fairly accurate model of the scheme. By photographing many views at various angles of lighting (representing different times of day), we were able to make a precise determination of the best angle of view to show as much of as many of the buildings as possible.

A computer model of the project would have provided almost the same freedom of investigation, but without quite the ease of simply moving around the physical model with a single-lens reflex camera. In addition, a computer-generated wireframe would not help us determine lighting angles. A slide of the selected view of the model (shown here in the inset photograph) was rear-projected at a chosen drawing size onto a sheet of vellum and traced—with some revisions—then transferred to the final illustration board for additional detailing and finished rendering in Prismacolor pencil.

The fact that the drawing was a color original illustration and is represented here in a two-color version carries something of a disadvantage, unlike a retrocolor for which the black-and-white original image is coherent in its own terms. In this case, the values of the blue sky and water were considerably darker in the color version, conveying more drama and impact than the image presented here. This example provides a reminder that blue does not usually carry its relative value when photographed in black-and-white.

The finished drawing received more than the usual exposure to the public in the form of full-page color promotional advertisements carried in the general media within this country and abroad. Even though impressive model photographs were also available, the drawn illustration was deemed to be the more persuasive marketing device.

Miami, Florida
Pietro Belluschi & Associates
Exterior perspective
Prismacolor on Strathmore board
18" × 18"
Six days (1981)

This photograph by the author of the architect's model provided the base layout for the final drawing.

United Airlines/O'Hare Airport Development

These two drawings were part of a suite of five produced to describe a new terminal and headquarters for a major domestic airline at the nation's busiest airport. The drawings were executed on vellum with a watercolor paper underlay and were planned for eventual retrocoloring.

The subject of these drawings—a huge concourse to accommodate enormous numbers of people—is not generically inspiring. It resulted here in an architecture consisting of repetitive structural bays over a polished floor with crowds of people, who provide the principal elements of the drawing. There is some specificity and interest in the industrial-type detailing of this "skin and bones" approach to shelter. It seemed that the main task in these drawings was to give a sense of what was inside (under the opaque roof structure) and outside (a bright sky visible through glazed walls and skylights). We made a conscientious attempt to communicate the ambiance and scale of this essentially simple space.

When attempting to communicate scale at eye level, it is almost always important to use the most universal of scale devices, the human figure—or, in this case, many of them. The disposition of individuals and clusters of the crowd becomes an important compositional consideration in drawings such as these. Not only must figures be placed to avoid obscuring crucial architectural details (column-floor intersections, for example) but there should appear to be a certain randomness of figure and group location. This effect is not serendipity, and takes a fair amount of attention to achieve. Notice that in both pictures there is one figure closest to the observer—to enhance the depth of field— that the figure is nearly but not exactly centered in the format, and that it does not face the viewer, to minimize social distraction.

This type of textured, relatively coarse drawing may not be the most appropriate possible to represent this precise, high-tech variety of architecture. However, it could also be argued that the architectural and rendering styles relieve and complement each other. As usual, schedule was a prime consideration; consequently, the medium choice and resolution level were largely determined by the amount of time available to produce the five drawings.

Chicago, Illinois
Murphy/Jahn (O'Hare Associates)
Interior perspective (gallery)
Black Prismacolor on vellum with textural underlay
12″ × 19″
Six days (1983)

(page 122)
Interior perspective (main hall)
Black Prismacolor on vellum with textural underlay
12″ × 19″
Six days (1983)

Pitney Bowes Headquarters

The drawings that follow were commissioned to describe the design for the national headquarters of a major office-equipment manufacturer. Two views were clearly necessary because of the great difference in character between the water side of the building (page 124) and the land side (page 125). The site has many large trees and interesting rock outcroppings, around which the scheme was designed, but these are visible from only one side of the building. The winter season was chosen for the representation so that at least some of the building center would be visible through the dense branches in the water-side view.

The design relies on a certain rigor and precision for much of its impact, so the drawings are relatively highly resolved to communicate that character. The sculpture shown in both views is by Alexander Calder, and is not a part of the Pitney Bowes headquarters—it is actually located at MIT. The sculpture simply provides for this drawing a convenient and specific means to suggest the location, scale, and general character of a sculptural complement to the building.

The land-side view is, I believe, a particularly strong "no-frills" drawing of a powerfully simple design. Even the sky was omitted, not so much for the sake of schedule, but for the heightened contrast its absence offered between solid building and air. The format coherence may be somewhat compromised by this choice, as a drawing with some figuration in every square inch of format is usually more compositionally integrated, if less elegant or dramatic. Notice that the uncluttered grassy foreground, which is devoid of other perspective cues, diminishes in texture scale with distance from the viewer.

Stamford, Connecticut
I. M. Pei & Partners (H. Cobb)
(page 124)
Exterior perspective (water side)
Black Prismacolor on vellum drymounted to board
10″ × 17″
Eight days (1981)

(page 125)
Exterior perspective (land side)
Black Prismacolor on vellum drymounted to board
10″ × 17″
Seven days (1981)

Duke University Law School

This project was actually an addition to an existing building, but it was so extensive and so altered the character of the original structure that it became, in effect, a whole new design. Because of this it was seen as appropriate to show the entire building in a single drawing, something that required not necessarily a true aerial perspective, but an elevated, or stepladder, viewpoint. This kind of view allows description of the building elevations in an aspect not too dissimilar from eye level, while showing the whole extent of the roof—although at a sharply raked angle—from above. The two-dimensional area of elevations shown in this picture is intended to exceed the area of roof forms slightly.

The actual orientation of the building severely limited the selection of a satisfactory sun angle. We finally decided to leave the principal (north-facing) wall just barely in shade. The almost-raking sun angle does highlight the tops of the fin columns nicely along the bowed form on the right side of the building. Our delineation of the precise array of shadow definition in the drawing was aided by photographs of a small model lighted from the same early morning sun angle.

We made use of several of our standard and dependable rendering devices in this drawing. To illustrate the elevation, we scored the thin mullions and used other linear indications. Graded resolution leaves the surrounding site as only vaguely suggested by coarsely textured value. Given the extensive amount of surrounding foliage, this device seemed appropriate, although with additional time and information we might have shown a bit more of the campus context in the background.

The selection of the foreground sculpture piece was left to the illustrator, which is a fairly common practice. We chose a Hadzi work entitled "The Three Bishops" that is actually sited adjacent to the now-existing Dallas Centre project, in lieu of the Lipschitz sculpture shown in our drawing of that building.

Durham, North Carolina
Gunnar Birkerts & Associates
Aerial perspective
Black Prismacolor on vellum with partial textural underlay (retrocolored)
12" × 18"
Six days (1985)

126

Westport Public Library

This type of simple linear or "extruded" interior space lends itself particularly to axial or one-point perspective illustration. By placing the all-important end wall parallel to the picture plane, the resulting representation is a true elevation with the least possible graphic ambiguity. The sloped ceiling and vertical walls on the left and right form angles in the drawing that correspond exactly to the actual ones in construction. Even though there are no other linear cues to the slant of the planar ceiling as it approaches the foreground, there is little question in a viewer's mind about constancy of plane or slope.

The selection of the specific station point was a simple matter after the axial perspective decision was made. In order to minimize distortion, the viewpoint/vanishing point should be located near the center of the space, exactly as is the case in a section perspective. In fact, this view could easily be transformed into a section perspective by introducing a cut plane in the foreground. This stepladder view was facilitated by the presence of a mezzanine from which this upper-floor eye-level picture was taken. The high viewpoint offers a nice opportunity to see the reflective tops of the bookshelves, which give a certain relief to the somewhat coarsely defined matte surfaces of the space.

The resolution level of the drawing is not high, but the simplicity of forms makes fineness of image grain less necessary than with extensive or complex subjects. I sometimes prefer the sketchy, vigorous quality of a highly textured drawing such as this or the Miami World Trade Center piece shown earlier in this chapter. Here, showing the effect of the space's natural lighting was a principal concern, and a granular representation seems to make it easier to focus upon such general issues than would extremely high resolution drawings.

It could be said that this drawing falls somewhere between a value study and a final presentation piece. Since the spontaneity and verve of a value study is frequently more compelling in a visceral sense than a final piece, it may be argued that a drawing should carry the lowest level of resolution possible while communicating the appropriate information about the drawn object.

Westport, Connecticut
Gwathmey Siegel & Associates
Interior perspective
Black Prismacolor on Strathmore board
11" × 17"
Four days (1982)

Library Square Development

This drawing of the top of a proposed seventy-story tower for Los Angeles is unusual for my office in virtually every respect. We typically work in a small (24-inch maximum) format and this one was over five feet tall. We virtually always employ some kind of verifiable perspective (constructed, computer-generated, or photographed) and this image is not a perspective at all, but a 45 degree oblique paraline drawing—although it is universally and incorrectly referred to as axonometric, which requires a different type of projection.

The drawing is a color original, with wax-base colored pencil applied in a nongraded and opaque fashion rather than in our usual highly graded transparent manner. The original base image was a mounted mural-paper photograph of a computer-generated line printout. The overall effect of the final drawing in color is schematic, two-dimensional, and almost posterlike; usual work is more representational, illusionistic, and photographic.

Normally there would have been a great deal of gradation of sky and building from top to bottom (or middle, in this case) but this drawing shows no color or value change whatever from the uppermost to the lowest range of windows. The value and chroma does change around the cylindrical structure, based on the amount of sky reflected by the windows at various angles to the line of view. This variation is achieved through the use of four different blue pencils, not by our usual method of lighter and heavier application of the same pencil. Some conditions of glazing and the way it is viewed (against the sky at the top, for instance) were graphically simplified to be consistent with the schematic nature of the rest of the drawing.

Naturally, some of the visual impact and drama of the highly saturated chromatic original is diminished in this black-and-white reproduction. As was the case with the Miami Center drawing, the blue areas of window and sky lost the most in translation, and are seen here as considerably less powerful in value than in the original version.

Los Angeles, California
I. M. Pei & Partners (H. Fredenburgh)
Exterior paraline drawing
Prismacolor on photomural paper
60" × 24"
Eight days (1985)

This aerial photomontage by Barry Zauss shows the tower in the context of the city of Los Angeles. (Photograph © Barry Zauss & Associates.)

130

6 Foreign Projects

Tehran Library Proposal (Competition)

This tiny (7- × 9-inch) drawing was made small for purposes of speed and economy. A couple of friends with a small budget and high hopes wanted some help with their competition entry, so I intentionally limited the scope of work by means of size. Size reduction meant increasing the resolution level, so I chose Mylar as a base, as it is the most finely grained drawing surface commonly available.

The perspective layout was very precisely constructed, and most of the rendering was done under a magnifier, to accommodate the size and resolution requirements. A Verithin pencil was used in some areas because of its greater hardness and ability to hold a sharp point longer than a Prismacolor can. Only one side of the Mylar surface was used for the drawing, even though the film was matte on both sides.

The scheme, as is frequently true with competitions, was pure and uncompromising—even polemical. This "no-frills" drawing (see also the Pitney Bowes drawing in the previous chapter) was intended to communicate the distilled, almost academic character of the design. No foreground, no sky, few figures, and only sparse vegetation were suggested—the pure, crystalline form of the building in light with the mountains in the background constitute the entire drawing.

Light, therefore, was the key element in defining this spare, isolated form. Much of the visible underside of the structure is in shade, with horizontal soffits lighted by "ground bounce." The darkness allows the skylights formed by the omission of an occasional cube to be clearly seen and understood. Glazing is treated here as totally transparent, defined only by mullions, which in reality would have to be much larger and more frequent. This drawing—along with the Portland Museum section perspectives and a few others—seems to communicate in a very direct way an intense and almost purely architectonic notion. Unfortunately, neither this nor any other design submitted in the competition was actually constructed, owing to Iran's turbulent history in the ensuing years.

Tehran, Iran
John Howey Associates with Carl Abbott
Exterior perspective view
Black Prismacolor and Verithin pencil on Mylar
7″ × 9″
Two days (1977)

Al Salaam Arcade

This interior drawing of a multistory mixed-use arcade in Kuwait shows a very narrow, long space, which made our choice of an axial perspective almost unavoidable. The space is intentionally designed narrow and high as a means of controlling the harsh sunlight common to that part of the world. For this project, we reluctantly abridged our long-standing rule about assuming overcast skies when a space frame or other intricately mullioned skylight is in the picture. Although Kuwait may have occasional overcast days, it is hardly a normal condition and therefore should probably not be shown.

The shadows generated by the vaulted skylight mullions are simplified indeed, since we broke a second house rule against showing light falling parallel to the picture plane in a one-point perspective. By moving the sun just to this side of the picture plane, the surfaces normal to our view (bridges, columns, and so on) barely receive raked light, but the shadows of the curved skylight mullions are close enough to straight lines to be represented as such.

The general tones of the surfaces in the arcade are made intentionally dark to emphasize the brilliance of the light outside. Lightness is reflected in the intermittent glazing, particularly where our view rakes it sharply on the right side. Without this glazing and the attention paid to reflections in it, the drawing would be much less graphically varied and effective. The ubiquitous drawing devices of scoring and aura were used in the floor pattern and bridges, respectively. The body of water shown beyond is, I believe, rendered a bit too dark and its horizon is more precisely defined than it would actually appear.

The scale figures shown in traditional Arab dress provide an example of the kind of double or even triple service that drawn figures can provide. Besides imparting a sense of scale and concentration of activity, these suggest the global location of the project as well. Foliage, scattered throughout the arcade in built-in planters, provides some sense of coolness and relief from the heat one can easily imagine feeling in this place.

Kuwait City, Kuwait
I. M. Pei & Partners (H. Fredenburgh)
Interior perspective
Black Prismacolor on vellum
11" × 17"
Four days (1978)

King Faisal Air Force Academy

The long, repetitive, semienclosed barracks court described here is shown in noncentered axial perspective because of its length, although this is a predominantly horizontal rather than vertical space. Both the sunlit and shade sides needed to be included, although not equally, in the picture. In such situations, it is easiest and causes the least distortion to use one-point perspective.

One compositional pitfall of this type of layout is the visual dominance of the linear convergence, which draws the eye inexorably toward the single vanishing point. By arranging the view to include some secondary centers of interest (the sunlit fountain, and the group of cadets playing ball), we intended to mitigate the visual demand of the many converging lines. An additional attempt to achieve this is introduced by the long horizontal underside of the bridge shown at the top of the picture in the foreground. Even though this visible piece of bridge is notably without perceptual cues, since neither end intersection is shown, the repetition of other bridges is so rhythmic and constant that the viewer has little doubt as to its identity.

The design for the building was in a fairly early stage when these illustrations were made. Thus, we did not need too high a level of resolution, and decided to use vellum with a textural underlay with sepia Prismacolor. This use of a single nonblack pencil limited the value range and softened the images to some extent, but imparted a pleasant warmth to the originals, slides, and color prints.

We used the same media in our exterior drawing of the entire project, shown in the inset. The exterior view suggests the isolation of the site, and makes apparent at least one of the reasons for the inward orientation of the living quarters. At one point in the design process, the large roof forms were considered to serve as water storage towers, in order to ensure a ready water supply in this arid and politically volatile corner of the world.

Al Kharj, Saudi Arabia
Arthur Erickson Architects
Exterior perspective
Prismacolor on vellum with partial textural underlay
11½" × 16½"
Four days (1980)

This drawing by the author shows a general eye-level view of the entire academy complex.

Austral Lineas Aereas Headquarters Proposal

Precision and reflectivity were the prime graphic considerations for representing this fine but rather uncharacteristic I. M. Pei design for a South American airlines headquarters. The architect's request was to "make it as shiny as a car," so reflections in the mirror glass were drawn with virtually the highest resolution possible for this medium.

As was the case with the Fountain Place drawing, we needed to add some specific sky clouding to communicate the specular reflectivity of the façade. Note that some cloud reflections in the glazing are situated so as to be cropped by the edge of the building—a condition possible only with reflectivity, not transparency (we did not want it to appear as though the viewer was looking *through* the building).

Because of the high level of resolution, we were able to show reflections of straight edges (the unseen building to the left, and the building's own interreflections) as slightly irregular and discontinuous at the butt-glazed joints. This subtlety suggests the usual imperfection of reflected images in actual glazing, but can be accomplished in pencil only with great care and a considerable investment of time.

The second material constituting the building, structural steel painted white, is shown with no less care than is the glazing. Illustrating thin, small shadow areas on white members is tricky, as there is a tendency to render the shadows too dark—particularly on the underside of the upper flange. That surface is bleached by a very strong light bounce from the white upper surface of the lower flange. At least these white surfaces were intended to be matte—delineating shiny white surfaces, such as Pei's MIT Arts and Media Technology building, is even more difficult.

The most graphically rich and geometrically interesting few square inches of the entire format occur in the structure's second bay from the right. This area of dense, almost infinite interreflection of the various building planes forms a compelling center of visual interest in the drawing, as it would, I believe, have done in the actual building as well. Unfortunately, bankruptcy eventually prevented the building from being constructed, so we can only speculate, on the basis of this drawing, how the headquarters would have appeared.

Buenos Aires, Argentina
I. M. Pei & Partners (I. M. Pei)
Exterior perspective
Black Prismacolor on vellum drymounted to board
20" × 30"
Nine days (1980)

Australian Parliament Building Proposal (Competition)

The presentation requirements for this international competition included two large (30- × 40-inch) original drawings of the proposed scheme, one aerial and one nonaerial view. The size requirements posed something of a problem, particularly for the lower view, shown on page 142.

First, the stepladder (or slightly above eye-level) viewpoint we decided to use shows a very long, horizontal bulding image that had to be related somehow to the required 30 × 40 format. Since we saw Australia as a big, wide-open country, we decided to show an enormous sky rather than extensive foreground. The first rule of composition would recommend that we *not* divide the format equally between earth and sky in any case. The diagonally graded area of sky tone also provided an opportunity for a rather dramatic counterchange of value between the stepped walls on the right and left. Since we normally work with small originals for ease of value tuning (among other reasons), the large format presented an unaccustomed difficulty. Tuning such a huge sky would ordinarily require us to step back from the original periodically during the drawing process to see the effect from a distance. I avoided that necessity by hanging a large mirror at an appropriate angle on a far wall and tuning the sky while seated *behind* the original, watching the image of my moving pencil on its face and correcting the drawing accordingly. This admittedly bizarre arrangement allowed continuous viewing of the drawing at an effective distance of thirty feet (twice the fifteen feet to the mirror) while actually working on it. Of course, the image of my pencil motion was reversed, but with a little practice I soon overcame that minor inconvenience.

The aerial view, shown opposite, was simply drawn as a cut-in photomontage, similar to several others in this book. Instead of having to deal with twelve hundred square inches of drawing format, I could spend the limited time available concentrating on the one hundred or so that actually constituted the proposal. This arrangement also ensured that the surrounding context of the city of Canberra was shown accurately, currently, and in considerable detail by the photograph that was supplied with the competition brief.

Canberra, Australia
Brown Daltas & Associates
Aerial perspective (photomontage)
Black Prismacolor on Strathmore board with mounted photographic print
30″ × 40″
Two days (1979)

(page 142)
Exterior perspective
Black Prismacolor on Strathmore board
30″ × 40″
Four days (1979)

BBC Headquarters Proposal

The image on the following two pages is a rendered orthographic representation of the Foster Associates' proposal for an expanded BBC facility in central London. Although it is unusual for this office to work in the Beaux-Arts form of rendered elevation, it seemed the appropriate vehicle here to establish the scale relationship firmly between this large proposed building and its historic surroundings. An orthographic drawing can show more directly than a perspective the actual heights of adjacent buildings in comparison to the new one, as well as their distances from it.

Two buildings in particular were considered to be very important neighbors of the new structure, the venerable All Souls church by John Nash (identifiable by the steeple) and the existing BBC headquarters immediately to the right of the proposed building. These existing buildings, along with the others shown here, were photographed extensively and in various lighting contexts specifically for this drawing. We decided to show them in their current state of weathering, complete with streaking, stains, and "urban patina" rather than idealize their images.

The proposed structure itself is a situationally designed mass, largely filling the available site and zoning envelope. The mass is divided by a glazed interior street oriented to align with the All Souls steeple. The site elevation becomes a section (or actually an interior elevation) of the new building since the section line occurs within the interior street. Crowds of scale figures are used to suggest the street's accessibilty and activity as a public circulation connector. There were proposed and drawn additional sub-basement studio spaces that are deleted in this image.

The main compositional strategy used here predicates diminishing contrast toward the far ends of the drawing. The proposed building itself, although central, is shown in fairly low contrast as well, partly because this image was actually in progress when design changes were occurring continuously. Since the drawing was made on drafting film, erasure was not a technical problem, only one of time and budget. As is typical with non-poché site sections, the coherence of this drawing is aided by the introduction of a substantial ground line, which helps to relate the parade of disparate buildings shown here.

London, England
Foster Associates
(pages 144–145)
Section perspective
Black Prismacolor on polyester drafting film
12″ × 14″
Six days (1985)

Retfotib Tower Proposal

The design of this office tower, which was to be located on a prime site on the main boulevard of Mexico City, dates from those relatively halcyon days prior to the recent oil-price crash and Mexico City's devastating earthquakes. The possibility of its construction now appears dim indeed, leaving this drawing as a main record of the I. M. Pei design.

As is usual for a building with a reflective façade—especially a faceted one such as this—it was important to adopt a sky divided into light and dark quadrants, so the facets reflecting them could be sharply defined against each other. It is characteristic of reflective materials in an angular relationship to be seen as having very high contrast—much higher than the same facets in a matte material, which rely only on incident sunlight and shadow for value variation. Note also in the glazed façade that there is a great deal of value gradation from dark at the top to light at the bottom, which is consistent with the sky it reflects.

The mutual interreflections in the façade heighten the perception of the sharp, crisp angularity that characterizes the mirror-glazed skin of the building. Some surrounding low buildings are shown reflected fractionally in the glazing, as is the gilded angel atop the column. In the retrocolored version of the drawing, the angel reflection is more apparent since it shows a glint of gold in the building façade.

Potential foreground distraction was minimized, and contrast reduced, one might say, by the presence of a convenient cloud shadow spreading over the near ground plane. The texture generated by the vellum is allowed to remain quite coarse in the street and crosswalk area in the lower portion of the format. The palm trees were drawn using a technique that makes pencil the perfect medium for such application. The secret is always to stroke the palm leaves quickly and *away* from the branch and the trunk in order to get the characteristic palmlike feathering of the fronds.

Mexico City, Mexico
I. M. Pei & Partners (I. M. Pei)
Exterior perspective
Black Prismacolor on vellum drymounted to board (retrocolored)
22″ × 17″
Eight days (1980)

Parcel Eight Development Proposal (Competition)

This detail drawing of a design submitted for an international competition shows only a fraction of the twin-tower scheme in order to concentrate attention at the pedestrian level, and on the geometrically complex tessellation at the bases of the towers. This selective drawing predates a similar one showing the base of the MGF Tower in Midland, Texas, which we eventually had to extend to full height by way of a graft onto the original drawing. Happily, one is insulated from that kind of request in the case of a competition submission.

As was the case with the Dallas Centre drawing (see chapter 4), the mutual interreflections between the glazing of the two adjacent towers is the main area of challenge and interest. Unlike the Dallas Centre project, however, the reflecting windows of the "eroded' part of the bulding are constantly changing planes, which results in a complex "wrinkled" reflected image of the opposite building. The reflecting faces in the main shaft of the towers are coplanar, and therefore simpler to construct and understand. It should be noted that the glass plane is recessed, which has the effect of doubling the reveal depth through reflection. This has a great influence on the left face of both towers, neither of which shows any sky reflection because of the recessed glazing.

The composition of this drawing is, I believe, exceptionally strong, with the large, stepped, low wall to the left recalling the crystalline setbacks of the tower bases. The traditional clear-day sky (darker at the top) works well here, providing a large, simple trapezoid of quiet value against which the intricacy of the building is foiled. The sky merges with the light value at the base of the left tower—a pleasant and unexpected subtlety that in no way compromises the legibility of the building form.

The foreground is treated schematically, showing no traffic but providing a solid graphic base for the drawing. A slight reflectivity is introduced in the paving and plaza for a touch of interest, and to suggest the feeling of freshness that follows an urban rain shower.

Republic of Singapore
Moshe Safdie & Associates
Exterior perspective
Black Prismacolor on vellum
12½" × 18"
Six days (1980)

Government Service Insurance System Headquarters

This aerial view of TAC's design for a huge low-rise governmental building in the Philippines is a straightfoward drawing of a very extensive object. In order to show the whole project, the station point had to be located hundreds of yards away and at a considerable altitude as well. Because of the distances, usual scale devices such as figures become invisible, leaving cars, buses, and even a freighter (at the extreme right side of the drawing) to give a sense of scale to the building.

The selection of the station point was, as is often the case, crucial to the satisfactory pictorial composition and description of the building. Because of the complexity and angularity of the building's plan, its aspect changes drastically from one viewpoint to another. In many views the parti seems ungainly and awkward from an elevated viewpoint. It was especially helpful that a reasonably current model of the scheme was available, which we were able to photograph selectively, much in the manner of the Miami Center project described in chapter 5.

This particular elevated viewpoint seems to explain the building adequately and yet shows it in a fairly tightly composed configuration. Notice that the angularity of the building is slightly simplified and related to the rectangular format by having one set of edges (the far sides of the upper roof decks) in parallel alignment with the horizon—and, therefore, with the top of the picture. The canal in the background is also parallel, which further marries the described object to its format.

The canal and other site surroundings were drawn softly in order to focus attention on the proposed structure, as well as to save time. The site elements were kept artificially dark (with the exception of the sky-reflecting water at the upper right side) as a value foil to highlight the building. Scoring was useful here in showing the extensive trellises and such details as flagpoles and markings of tennis courts. The drawing was ultimately enlarged photographically on mural paper, mounted, and retrocolored for presentation.

Manila, Philippines
The Architects Collaborative (H. Elkus)
Aerial perspective
Black Prismacolor on Strathmore board (retrocolored)
14" × 26"
Eight days (1983)

National Gallery Addition Proposal (Competition)

This is a drawing of Henry N. Cobb's competitive proposal for a major addition to London's National Gallery. The view was taken from an eye-level station point located in Trafalgar Square, with a center of vision through the proposed addition, but including much of the existing building context to each side. The right-hand third of the picture, which shows about half of the existing National Gallery building, is especially important, since it shows the main building to which the addition is being appended. The demarcation between the old Gallery building and the new was intentionally blurred, as it was the intent of the architect to achieve a high level of compatibility with the original building through the classical design of the new wing.

Although we had a good full-size photograph from this viewpoint to use in describing the existing buildings, there was scaffolding (as always) and traffic obscuring much of what we wanted to see, which required us to draw from building elevations as well. We juggled traffic, moving a double-decker bus into the foreground to serve as an additional cue that this was indeed London. The hazy, slightly overcast sky and soft shadows seemed to be characteristically English as well.

The part of the drawing devoted to the actual addition was, as usual, slightly higher in resolution than the rest of the picture. Value delineation or tone drawing seemed an effective means of showing the gentle curvature of the main cylindrical form of the addition in the soft light. We strove for a certain subtlety in describing the dark interior spaces visible through the two doorways facing us, avoiding simple black holes and suggesting something of the interior form. The intermittent openings above the cornice show a faceted upper-story element terminating in a sloped octagonal roof with a small lantern skylight at the top.

In a textbook example of designing on the final drawing, the decision to add the lantern skylight was made (after several tracing-paper overlays) during the final hour, when the drawing had been in process for a month. In defense of this designing method, I believe that it is more sensible to make certain design decisions based on an image of the building from an actual future viewpoint in its urban context than to do so while looking at some isolated elevation or axonometric line drawing.

London, England
Henry N. Cobb with I. M. Pei & Partners
Exterior perspective
Black Prismacolor on Strathmore board
11" × 20"
Ten days (1986)

Grand Louvre Facilities Expansion

Few cultural institutions in the Western world are as hallowed as the Grand Louvre in Paris. When it became necessary to expand the facilities of this venerable edifice, controversy was sure to attend any proposal requiring a visible reordering or addition of elements. For that and other reasons, complete veracity was required to represent the proposed new skylight and entry to the expanded underground facilities. Computer-generated perspectives, provided by Computervision, Inc., were used to show the size and proportions of the new glazed pyramid in relation to the existing pavilions from numerous eye-level viewpoints. The machine-plotted constructions were also used to verify the hand-constructed bases for each of the drawings. In addition, the drafted constructions were typically cross-checked for accuracy by no fewer than five independent methods.

The day and night views shown on the following pages depict the glazed pyramid's two kinds of character when it is predominantly reflective and transparent. The pyramidal form was chosen partly because the reflections seen in the daytime would almost entirely consist of images of the sky—not of the surrounding building—because of the slope of the glazing. The nighttime view shows the nearer structural members as backlighted, while suggesting the brightly illuminated structure inside. Design revisions subsequent to these drawings have refined and reduced the interior structure to a gossamer fineness, which was facilitated by the innate structural stability of the pyramid form.

The composition of the day and night views posed exactly the same problem as for the first drawing in this book (the Dracut project) since the building image consists of a narrow, horizontal band centered in the rectangular format necessary for publication purposes. In the daytime view a rather turgid Parisian sky was added to fill out the rectangle, and the dependable illustration device of wet pavement was introduced into the night view. The searchlight beams and their reflections added welcome vertical elements, recalling the similar lights used on occasion at the Place de l'Etoile located at the far end of the Champs-Elysées.

Paris, France
I. M. Pei & Partners (I. M. Pei)
Exterior perspective (Mollien Pavilion)
Black Prismacolor on Strathmore board
17½" × 24"
Eleven days (1984)

(Page 156)
Exterior perspective (day view)
Black Prismacolor on Strathmore board
12½" × 17"
Four days (1984)

(page 157)
Exterior perspective (night view)
White Prismacolor on black museum board
12½" × 17"
Three days (1984)

This computer-generated wireframe perspective was one of hundreds used to study and explain the design of the pyramid.

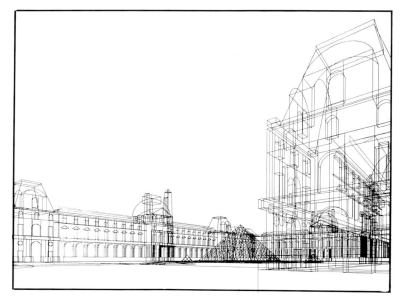

INDEX